AMERICA Shattered

Unmasking the Plot to Destroy Our Families and Our Country

TEXE MARRS

LTP Living Truth Publishers
8103 Shiloh Court • Austin, Texas 78745

OTHER BOOKS BY TEXE MARRS

NEW AGE CULTS AND RELIGIONS

MILLENNIUM: Peace, Promises and the Day They Take Our Money Away

RAVAGED BY THE NEW AGE: Satan's Plan to Destroy Our Kids

MYSTERY MARK OF THE NEW AGE: Satan's Design for World Domination

DARK SECRETS OF THE NEW AGE: Satan's Plan for a One World Religion

MEGA FORCES: Signs and Wonders of the Coming Chaos

AMERICA SHATTERED: Unmasking the Plot to Destroy Our Families and Our Country

Copyright © 1991, by Texe Marrs. Published by Living Truth Publishers, a division of Living Truth Ministries, 8103 Shiloh Court, Austin, Texas 78745.

Scripture quotations are from the King James Version of The Holy Bible.

Cover Design: Texe Marrs, Sandra Schappert and Terrell Powell.

Printed in the United States of America.

Library of Congress Catalog Number 90-61915

ISBN 0-9620086-6-4

CONTENTS

INTRODUCTION

Today, the New Age movement has infiltrated all areas of our daily lives. Because of its pervasive influence, our families are rapidly being undermined, and our children are falling into bondage to dark forces. The Bible clearly tells us that in the last days the family will become an endangered species. Youth will no longer honor and respect parents and their elders. Brother will go against brother. Mothers and fathers will not possess natural affection. In sum, chaos will reign in human relationships. And this fits in perfectly with the devil's grand strategy.

My goal in this book is to awaken Christians everywhere to the insidious working of the New Age plan and the aim of its backers to wreck our families. Only through knowledge of the Truth—and by understanding the dangers—can we confront this damaging assault on family values.

Though the men and women of the New Age have, regrettably, so far been successful in their campaign against the family, there is no reason for us as Christian believers to be distraught or dismayed. With God's power in our lives, we have victory. He is able to protect you and me and to put up an impenetrable barrier of protection between the forces of destruction and our families. His love will never fail.

Texe Marrs
Austin, Texas

PART I

Spiritual Warfare and the Processing of Humanity

Is it strange to believe that a determined group of evil plotters seeks to overthrow America and merge this nation into a One World Government? Is it difficult to conceive that this same Plot has targeted our families for destruction?

Frankly, five years ago, when I first began my in-depth study and investigation of the New Age movement and the secret societies which oversee New Age activities and operations, I was not fully aware of the horrendous dimension of the danger that we now face. Still, the Bible forewarns us that in the last days, the devil, knowing that he has but a short time, will be furious. He and his demon spirits will, the Bible reveals, go all out to possess and inhabit peoples everywhere.

According to Revelation 13, he will make war against the saints. In Revelation 17, we find that the devil will succeed in a mind-boggling conspiracy to control the very minds and wills of all the political leaders throughout planet Earth. He will succeed, that is, *until* finally, Jesus Christ Himself returns to put things right and set up His millennial kingdom (Revelation 19-22).

Spiritual Warfare Against the Family

This, then, is *spiritual warfare*, directed especially against believers in Christ. Moreover, it is a particularly virulent form of spiritual warfare that, in fact, encompasses the entire globe. America is the primary target, however, for today it is American culture and American religious ideas that dominate the world.

The family, because it is ordained by God, is the very core and bulwark for any nation. A strong family unit translates into a strong and enduring America. On the other hand, if an enemy were to set out to *conquer* a nation, his best objective would be the destruction and dissolution of its families. *As the family goes, so goes the nation.*

A pitifully weakened and helpless America is a nation that can be easily integrated into a New World Order. Thus, the devil and his demons constantly conduct spiritual warfare against the Christian family. The Christian family is the dike that protects America from an all consuming, onrushing flood. Punch holes in the dike, or better yet, dismantle it entirely, and America is lost.

The Plot Unmasked

America Shattered is not only a documented account of an unholy plot to undermine the family and thereby subvert, transform and take over our country, it is also a *Spiritual Warfare Manual* for concerned Christians. This important book is for Christians who believe the Bible when it tells us that since the days of Mystery Babylon, there has existed a conspiracy by the devil to stifle, immobilize and strangle God's people.

This book is for discerning men and women who refuse to give in to the devil's modern-day goal of One World Religion and Government. And it is for vigilant, dedicated parents who are well aware that the devil's foolhardy war on the family is simply one more strategy in Satan's ill-fated, ill-conceived last days campaign to oust God from His heavenly throne.

The Apostle Paul described the devil's conspiracy as a secretive campaign, so well organized and so deeply hidden and undercover, that, finally, almost all the world would be taken in and deceived. He warned of a *strong delusion* to come that would blind all who do not know Jesus Christ as Lord. And he spoke of the "Mystery of Iniquity," an evil but masterfully orchestrated Plan which only the elect will be able to understand and successfully confront.

According to Paul, in the last days there would come a "falling away" from the Truth, and then the antichrist is to step forward onto the final stage of history. Thus, the ages-old conspiracy will reach its final, ultimate pinnacle just before Christ Himself comes to bring Satan's shaky house of cards crashing down. Here's how the Apostle Paul described these events:

> *For the mystery of iniquity doth already work: only he who now letteth will let, until he be taken out of the way. And then shall that Wicked be revealed, whom the Lord shall consume with the spirit of his mouth, and shall destroy with the brightness of his coming: Even him, whose coming is after the working of Satan, with all power and signs and*

lying wonders, And with all deceivableness of unrighteousness in them that perish; because they received not the love of the truth, that they might be saved.

And for this cause God shall send them strong delusion, that they should believe a lie: That they all might be damned who believed not the truth, but had pleasure in unrighteousness.

But we are bound to give thanks always to God for you, brethren beloved of the Lord, because God hath from the beginning chosen you to salvation through sanctification of the Spirit and belief of the truth (II Thessalonians 2:7-13).

So we know that the devil and his companion evil spirits are working feverishly today to wreck everything that is righteous and holy. There is and has always been a conspiracy and a plot by demonic powers: "For we wrestle not against flesh and blood, but against principalities, against powers, against the rulers of the darkness of this world, against spiritual wickedness in high places" (Ephesians 6:12).

Many people today, rejecting the clear Word of God, disbelieve in supernatural beings. These are mere old wives' tales and fables, they say. But Jesus knew what Satan is all about. He testified that there *is* a devil, and that he is "a liar, and the father of it" (John 8:43-44). Jesus cast out demon spirits from possessed people, and He Himself was personally tempted by the devil in the wilderness. Notably, as an example for us, Christ *used scripture* as His only weapon of spiritual warfare--and what a weapon it was! "It is written," He reminded the Evil One, and the devil shrank from hearing the Word.

The Human Dimension of Evil

While most people too quickly reject the reality of the devil and his demons and too readily scoff at the reality of an ages-old plot and conspiracy, strangely, some who *do believe* the Bible's clear teachings on supernatural warfare fail to recognize that there are *human beings* who also are involved in this latter days conspiracy. When it comes to the reality of human beings being involved on the devil's side in such a plot, they are prone to discount it. "Surely, there can't be a *human conspiracy* at large in the world," they scoff, "How ridiculous!"

These skeptics are ignorant of scripture and even of human history. Again, we have the authority of God's Word as testimony. For example, Paul tells us that *in the latter days* there will be ". . . false apostles, deceitful workers, transforming themselves into the apostles of Christ. And no marvel; for Satan himself is transformed into an angel of light. Therefore, it is no great thing if his ministers also be transformed as the ministers of righteousness; whose end shall be according to their works" (II Corinthians 11:13-15).

This, then, we can conclude with certainty: the devil chooses *human leaders* to serve as ministers for his great but evil work. Such people coordinate and execute his plots; and they, in turn, are personally led by demons in carrying out their ungodly task:

13

*Now the Spirit speaketh expressly, that in the latter
times some shall depart from the faith, giving heed
to seducing spirits, and doctrines of devils;
Speaking lies in hypocrisy; having their conscience
seared with a hot iron (I Timothy 4:1-2).*

Are New Age Disciples Demon Possessed?

From my observations and from the insight given me by
God to accomplish my work in exposing this latter day
plot, I am convinced that *most* human leaders in Satan's
network of co-conspirators are either *obsessed* or *possessed*
(that is, inhabited and controlled) by demons (see Matthew
8:24-34 and Mark 5:2-18).

Demon obsession or *control*, with or without actual
possession, is no doubt how the devil is able to sway the
minds of the masses. It is not generally understood that
demon spirits are quite adept at controlling and manipulating
the thoughts of peoples' minds. Most people today are
defenseless because they do not have God in their hearts
and souls. This is why they are highly susceptible to mental
delusions, obsessions, insatiable desires, addictions,
confusion, unexplainable and compulsive behaviors,
depression, anxiety, and even psychiatric disorders that
baffle psychiatrists and medical doctors. Yet, few realize
the *spiritual* nature of their psychological and physical
problems. This is why the masses are fit candidates for
today's New Age propaganda and delusions.

How is the devil able to deceive so many, then? He does
so by organizing *demon spirits* in the unseen world. They,

in turn, train, inspire, supervise and guide *human leaders* of the conspiracy, instructing them on the fine points and on the methods and techniques, tactics and strategies of the ongoing "Mystery of Iniquity" (see II Thessalonians 2). These human leaders, in turn, recruit and/or *brainwash* the gullible *masses*: "In whom the god of this world (Satan) hath blinded the minds of them which believe not . . ." (II Corinthians 4:4).

In summary, we have a pyramidal structure of evil personages and spirits implicated in this incredible conspiracy and plot.

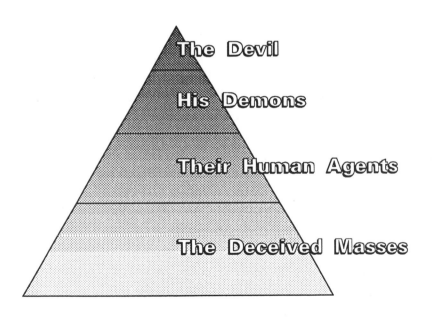

It is significant that the masses of this world are "blinded" by Satan. Amazing though it may be to the unwitting, the devil is described in the Bible as "god of this world!" Jesus, you'll remember, told Pilate that *His*, Christ's kingdom *is not* of this world. Someday, however, He will claim it as His own. Then He will cast the devil and his followers into the pit (see Revelation 19-22).

Meanwhile, those of us who are of God are already citizens of the Kingdom of God, for the Holy Spirit and Christ lives within us. Therefore, the *spiritual kingdom* is within us now, today.

Not so, however, for the unbeliever. He or she remains under the authority of the "god of this world," the devil, and only through God's grace is there hope of escape. The unbeliever is "blinded" so that the Truth cannot be seen or understood (see Daniel 12:10). Only if the Holy Spirit draws the lost person to Christ will his blindness be lifted.

Thus, the devil has successfully accomplished the "blinding" of the vast majority of Americans. He has perfected a unique technological system of *mind control* and *mass hypnosis*. It is this remarkable system that enables the devil to disorient and misdirect the masses, induce in their minds a strong delusion, and convince them that all is well, that black is white, that evil is good. I call the operation of this remarkable system of mind control and mass hypnosis *The Processing of Humanity*.

The Processing of Humanity: Mind Control in the Last Days

True Christians everywhere know that something is very, very wrong in the world around us. Something is horribly amiss. Something dreadful and terrible. Discerning Christians today feel a deep sense of foreboding, of impending horror. It is a feeling that while we are free through the grace of God, all around us are men, women, and children caught up as prisoners in some kind of strange and eerie twilight zone, frighteningly suspended in a gruesome, scary dimension not of their own choosing.

Each day, Americans are forced to undergo a severe form of mental and social shock. Our minds grow numb as we watch the TV news accounts of America's mass murderers--of a man, for example, in Milwaukee killing 17 unsuspecting victims and dismembering their bodies. Picking up the newspaper, we read of sadistic, vicious homosexuals and lesbians storming churches, flinging blood and condoms on altars and screaming curse words and epithets at stunned congregations who gape upon the outrageous spectacle from their pews.

We know that our youth are joining violent teen gangs and murdering each other out of sheer boredom and for thrills and "kicks." We watch, immobilized, as an entire generation is destroyed by the ravages of alcohol, cocaine and other illegal, mind-warping drugs. Yet, drug lords, pushers, and narcotic kingpins in Columbia, Burma, Mexico--and in the very streets of every city and town in our own nation--operate with impunity, often sneering at efforts by law enforcement to stop them.

Meanwhile, criminal activity is rampant and no one is safe anymore; no, not even in our own homes, behind our security locks and burglar alarms.

A Plague of Mind Control Imagery

Yes, something is terribly, terribly wrong. Still, few seem to be able to focus in on the root causes of our dilemma. Peoples' understanding is clouded and uncertain.

A book on euthanasia—on how to commit suicide—rockets to the top of the *New York Times* bestseller list. We are stunned, and confused. Why? How can this be?, we ask.

Pro-life groups report to us the grim statistics: over 25 million unborn babies slaughtered since the Roe vs. Wade Supreme Court decision in 1973. *Twenty-five million!* The number staggers the imagination. Yet, we seem gripped by a lack of will or a lack of knowledge of how to stop the carnage. So it continues, and more babies will die.

Movie theaters serve up the most blasphemous of movies, like *The Last Temptation of Christ*, which depicts Jesus as a whining idiot who carries on an affair with Mary Magdalene. We blink at the offense. Some protest, but to no avail. Seemingly, we can do nothing to stop such atrocities.

Even *Walt Disney*, the movie studio that gave us Donald Duck, Mickey Mouse, and so many other delightful characters, has moved our consciousness into this abominable new twilight zone. Now Disney offers us movies like *Ghosts*, to teach our youth how to communicate with the spirit world, and *The Dead Poets Society*, so they can be shocked numb by the scene of a young man who takes a pistol to his head and blows his own brain to bits.

Do Our Tax Dollars Go For Pornography and Blasphemy?

Our President, George Bush, says that he is on our side. He, too, is a "Christian." But then he demands, and gets, full funding from the U.S. Congress ($170 million in the last year alone) for The National Endowment For the Arts (NEA). As the president himself well knows, the NEA is a government agency that freely gives our taxpayer dollars away in grants to the most grotesque forms of art ever conceived. Yet, our "Christian" president insists that no restrictions be made on what is allowed to be produced with *our* money by NEA's generous chairman and its board.

The NEA has funded a painting of "Jesus" as a heroin addict. It has sponsored—with tax dollars—a gay rights film of "Jesus" giving "safe sex" instruction to gays and to young people, with our "Lord" demonstrating the proper use of condoms. The title: *Jesus Christ Condom*. There's also government money for Annie Sprinkle, a nude striptease "artist" who manipulates her female organs with a flashlight on stage, while, incredibly, gleefully bragging to the debauched audience that "The U.S. government is paying for this."

When frustrated Christians, such as the courageous Don Wildmon of the American Family Association, complained about NEA's dirty work, our own President George Bush, a self-professed Episcopal "Christian," stepped in to protect the NEA and its work. On national television Bush insisted to Congress and the public that the NEA and its chairman are "doing a good job." Newspapers and magazines across the nation then slur and ridicule

Wildmon and other concerned Christians, labeling them "censors" and "bigots"—and worse, for their stance in opposing taxpayer-funded pornography.

Indeed, something is wrong. Horrendously wrong. True Christians know it when they learn of the photos taken by a homosexual photographer, Robert Mapplethorpe, being proudly and arrogantly displayed in the finest museums in our largest cities. Christians are aghast and heart-stricken to learn that the photographs include unimaginable scenes of a young boy and girl being sexually abused, and images of brutal, monstrously immoral and sadist homosexuals urinating in the mouths of their gay lovers.

Filth is Constitutionally Protected

Yes, Christians are aghast, but then, what can they do? They are informed that all this is "freedom of expression," constitutionally protected "rights." Good for America. Worthwhile. Even a jury trial in Cincinnati, Ohio, affirms it. When the director of the local museum was put on trial for exhibiting the Mapplethorpe photo collection, the men and women of the jury returned with a verdict of "not guilty." So we cannot blame liberal judges for these horrors. The people themselves are demanding the right to revel in pornography, blasphemy, and similar evils.

According to the Cincinnati jury, the so-called "homoerotic art exhibit" *did not* violate "community standards of decency." And you know what? They were right. Today, such filth *does not* cut across the grain of the average American's moral standards. This is exactly what the majority in this country wants and is getting.

The Enslavement of Our Youth

Our youth continuously view graphic lesbian and other perverted sex on MTV. Their favorite rock stars gyrate to the staccato beat of drums and rabid twangs of electric guitars as they perform abnormal sex acts right on our TV screens! Moreover, our youth attend rock concerts at which altar calls are held for the devil and the name of Jesus is laughed at and cursed. Then they go on to buy and proudly wear T-shirts with the satanic logos and symbols of the rock group that has committed these vile acts.

Parents look on—and most do nothing. Most even approve. The few who do not are paralyzed. Spellbound. After all, they reason, what *can* we do?

In public school classrooms, society has moved from a court ruling excluding simple prayers to the enthusiastic teaching of witchcraft, New Age techniques, one world religionism, and a hatred for Christian ethics and values. Patriotism and love of country is scoffed at and derided. Globalism is praised.

Parents who protest are labeled "ignorant fundamentalists"—and deemed troublemakers. They're pointedly told, "It's none of your business," by angry teacher groups such as The National Education Association, and even by local PTA groups. Rejected parents crawl into their shells. Hurt. Confused. Perplexed. Saddened. There's nothing we can do, they conclude. Nothing.

Shadow Boxing Against An Unseen Foe

Yes, unmistakably, something is wrong. Monstrously so. True Christians are bewildered as to what to do. Most are held in check by invisible chains—strongly resilient, binding cords that resemble steel and iron in their rigidity.

I do not believe that the picture I am painting is exaggerated. Not at all. Bleak, yes, but exaggerated or far out? No.

True Christians everywhere are well aware that society has gone crazy. They know that some kind of unnamed, yet dark and lethal force has been unleashed in America and throughout the world. But they simply cannot figure out its nature, nor gauge its exact dimensions. They are befuddled . . . and worried.

Today, most Christians are like shadow boxers. They dimly perceive the faint shadow of a hidden opponent, an opponent who is hideous and frightful, life-threatening and ferocious. They want to fight, to do something about it . . . They are on the verge of reaching out, grasping hold, and struggling mightily against this unseen foe. But finally, most give up the effort. The foe is too wily, too smart and cunning. He's not to be had, he's not even able to be identified. He's a will-o'-the-wisp. A phantom.

And so, many true Christians, weary and bone-tired, soul-sick and anxious, sink back into the morass. No, they conclude, there's nothing I can do.

But they are wrong!

There is Something You and I Can Do!

My message in this book is for the true Christian, the discerning Christian. It is for the man or woman who cares about the Truth, who desperately wants the Word and loving grace of an Almighty God to reverberate around the globe. It is for the man or woman who is fed up with fighting shadows and is now ready to see the enemy for who he is and understand what he is up to. It is for Christian warriors who are determined to use every tool, every weapon, and every strategy available to them in order to thwart, defend against, and aggressively lock in combat the slippery foe.

My declaration to you is that there *is* something you can do. You *can know* who and what you are up against. You *can* identify and fight the enemy. And, with God's help, you *can* and *will be* victorious!

Later in this book we will examine specific ways we can fight back—and win—against the flood of New Age evil that today almost overwhelms us. In Parts V and VI, I outline a battle plan for Spiritual Warfare. I also reveal the little known fact that the entire New Age belief system is a fraud and a failure. I'll show that even America's top scientists have dismissed New Age psychology, techniques and methods as worthless and devoid of value. And I'll provide information on how Christians can use government agencies such as the Equal Employment Opportunity Commission (EEOC) to turn back the New Age tide.

But the first thing we must do in our fight against the growing darkness is to shed heavenly light on its plot to undermine and destroy the family. The attack on the family is massive and seems to be coming from all directions and from all quarters. There is a "battle plan" put together by the New Age and New World Order conspirators. Once we reveal and unmask their master Plan, then we can know how to best counter and defeat the conspirators who now are aligned against our families and our country.

PART II

The Late, Great Christian Family

And he had power to give life unto the image of the beast, that the image of the beast should both speak, and cause that as many as would not worship the image of the beast should be killed.
(Revelation 13:15)

Christianity and its churches . . . will wither away slowly, as the people die out of them, as the new religion gains . . .
Benjamin Creme
Tara Center

Our children will have to live with the New Age standards. Their parents, too, must comply. Those who do not will end up as unreconcilable outcasts.
Foster Bailey
Lucis Trust

The Masters of the New Age have a problem. A major problem. If they are to capture this entire nation, they know they have to first attack and destroy parents and family. The family unit will have to go. It is to be replaced by the concept of "Community."

25

The Community as a whole shall be custodian and guardian of our children. The Communists in Soviet Russia and Maoists in Red China call it the "State." They say that children belong not to their parents but to the state. New Age plotters substitute a more appealing and innocent-sounding term. They prefer the term *Community*.

New Age Evangelism: The Battle Plan

The New Age leadership has a finely detailed evangelistic battle plan, given by Satan, which they are now using to grab our kids and destroy our families. Its five major tactics are as follows:

1. Exalt "Community" as the basic unit of society.

2. Debase the family.

3. Dissolve parental authority and responsibility.

4. Scream, preach, and assert the rights of the child over the rights of the parents.

5. Set new "Community" standards to put pressure on and squeeze Christian parents between the teeth of a tight and vicious vise.

The New Age leadership is convinced that the final results of their Battle Plan tactics will be the total abolishment of the family as we have known it. Then, after the traditional family is dissolved and parents' rights are abrogated and thrown out, the children will be ripe for the taking. Defenseless, powerless, unprotected, they are to be savagely plundered. This is the awful strategy of Satan in these last days.

As a Christian parent, you need to be fully aware of this Plan. With adequate knowledge and spiritual discernment you can successfully prevent the New Age child abusers from grabbing your children. First of all, you must understand this vile New Age, Communist-oriented concept of "Community" and realize the evil that belies this serpentine word.

The "World Plan:" Providing the Perfect New Age Environment

In her astonishingly detailed book *When Humanity Comes of Age*, Vera Stanley Alder, a widely quoted New Age lecturer and writer, has an entire chapter entitled "Understanding the World Plan." Alder fervently believes in New Age goals. She preaches that the New Age Plan is to take young children from their first moment of birth and raise them in a "perfect" New Age society. Through the Plan, she writes, "man will eventually become perfect and God-like."[1]

Alder outlines in her book a number of The Plan's chief provisions for kids. The dimensions she reveals are chilling. It is important we examine just a few of the more frightening tenets of the mind-boggling New Age Plan for our families and kids.

First, Alder says that the One World Government set up by the coming New Age Christ and his top political officials will establish a Town and Country Planning Council to oversee and supervise the restructuring of communities across America and the world. Entire new communities will be set up in isolated areas and "people will be encouraged to move outward to the Model Community towns and villages."[2]

Each Community, Alder explains, will be self-contained. There will be one, massive, unified complex of buildings, all interconnected, with everything from medical and health facilities to cultural and recreation centers and schools. There will be "a single Community meals center" or cafeteria where all families will eat in common. The Community will have just *one* church because everyone will have one faith—the New Age World Religion. The same building used for the church will be used to house the courts and the police.[3]

Heaven on Earth. . . . Or a Concentration Camp?

In her book, Alder even includes a drawing of this ideal New Age Community. One glance at her dream-world fantasy, New Age utopia should be enough to shake up anyone who has not yet had their minds blinded by Satan. *Alder's blueprint for the ideal New Age Community resembles an architect's plan for a prison or even a concentration camp.*

In the architect's sketch or drawing for Alder's "perfect" New Age Community, there are no doors or exits to the outside, external world. There is no escape route and traffic is not allowed to move freely in and out of the Community.

New Age Concentration camps, or glorious, future communities?

(From Vera Stanley Alder's When Humanity Comes of Age, *New York, NY, Samuel Weiser, Inc., 1974)*

The only entrance and exit are by use of a ribbon train/rail system that looks suspiciously like a serpent in its construction.

In the ideal New Age Community, kids will not be able to play freely outdoors; they and their parents are forced to use whatever playground facilities are provided on the rooftops of the common buildings.

The Family Collective

The proposed New Age community is, in reality, obviously a prison and a confinement center where families will live as hostages, as indebted prisoners and locked-up slaves of their New Age captors. The shocking truth is that Alder's ideal New Age Community is a warmed over version of Communist China and Soviet Russia's "ideal" family collective. This becomes painfully apparent when we read Alder's dictum that: "Collective agriculture and collective industrial work should be the rule."[4]

According to the New Age Community regulations, food and agricultural surpluses will be turned in to a Surplus Pool and redistributed to other areas of the world where the need is greater. Naturally there will be a World Food Authority in charge of this redistribution.

A New Economic System

To complete the dreadful picture, let's take a look at Alder's plan for the *economy* in which our children are to be raised. She says that in the New Age world soon to come, *all money, all national currencies, will be abolished:*

> *As the bulk of commerce would be carried on by means of exchange, and individual needs would largely be supplied on the ration card system, the need for the handling of money would dwindle. . . . There would be a central 'bank' which decided the value or price of all goods produced. This value would probably be described in terms of letters and numbers, the letters representing the quality of work and materials and the numbers representing the hours of work entailed.*[5]

How horrifying! Vera Stanley Alder is considered by some in the New Age as one of the world's most eminent and highly regarded philosophers. Yet the economic system she has described as ideal perfectly fits the prophesied economic system of the last days Antichrist, the Beast with the number 666. In Revelation 13:15-18, we discover that the Antichrist will tyrannize and control the people by controlling the money system:

> *And he had power to give life unto the image of the beast, that the image of the beast should both speak, and cause that as many as would not worship the image of the beast should be killed.*

> *And he causeth all, both small and great, rich and poor, free and bond, to receive a mark in their right hand, or in their foreheads.*

And that no man might buy or sell, save he that had the mark, or the name of the beast, or the number of his name.

Here is wisdom. Let him that hath understanding count the number of the beast: for it is the number of a man; and his number is Six hundred threescore and six.

Children to be the Focus of Attention

Innocent children will no doubt be the chief victims in this scheme by New Agers to "encourage" the advanced countries' populations to leave their present homes, towns, and cities and set up residence in strictly controlled, New Age Communities.[6] Alder stresses that the child will be the focus of attention:

The first need will be to teach the child what he is, why he is, and what lies before him. If a vision and an ideal is held up to him in his earliest years, a foundation is laid.[7]

Other New Age theorists agree with Alder's desire to get hold of children as early as possible. "The younger the better," says Alice Bailey's spirit guide Djwhal Khul.[8] In her New Age classic, *Education for the New Age*, Bailey, founder of the Lucis Trust, recommends that opportunities be created "to train the child from its earliest breath."[9]

Children are to be Taught the New Age Religion Only

In the New Age Community, children are to be taught to believe in a religion of unity and community. They will be carefully trained to serve the "group will" rather than an external God. Adler states:

> *The child must be taught. . .the art of merging his effort and forgetting his ego in selfless group work for the good of all.*[10]

According to The Plan, the child will learn about a different religion than the narrow, separatist faith of his parents. He will learn to accept the more liberalized and collectivist New Age religion. Christianity will be replaced by a New Age World Religion that is based on bits and pieces of all religions. A composite New Age Bible will be developed by church leaders, and it will be used in place of the Christian Bible.[11]

The Plan provides that children are to be trained, step-by-step, into the "new truths" of the New Age religion. As explained by Benjamin Creme:

> *Christianity and its churches . . . will wither away slowly, as the people die out of them, as the new religion gains its adherents and exponents, and is gradually built by humanity.*[12]

"Our children" pronounces Foster Bailey, a leader of the Lucis Trust, "will have to live with the New Age standards." Their parents, too, must comply, Bailey warns. "Those who do not will end up as unreconcilable outcasts" of society.[13]

Foster Bailey assures us in his book *Things to Come* that "There is a Plan, God's Plan for man, and we shall know much more about that Plan in the New Aquarian Age than we have ever known before."[14]

No Separation of Church and State

Like Alder, Foster Bailey presents us with other outstanding features of the New Age Plan for our children. First, he reveals that the separation of church and state will end once the New Age "Christ" and leadership take control of governments. "Both government and religion," says Bailey, "should be interrelated in that which is good for *man.*"[15]

The merger of church and state will be easy to accomplish, Bailey suggests, once Christianity dies off or is destroyed and a unity-minded One World New Age Religion supplants it. He and other New Agers insist that only Christianity is now holding back and preventing this world unity. This is, they claim, why Bible-believing Christian churches must be eliminated in the New Age and kids brought up to believe in a new religion of unity. Bailey explains it this way:

> *Religions come and go. To cling to a church that perpetrates a religion that is no longer useful . . . is harmful to its followers as well as to the total human consciousness of spiritual values.*[16]

According to the New Age leadership, only if all vestiges of Biblical Christianity are erased can the Aquarian Age successfully develop a new civilization based upon deeper and better life values. The demise of Christianity, it is said, will result in a new religion with a God of love. The world finally will have a religion that will promote mental freedom and create right relations between men, nations, and races.

How to Raise Perfect New Age Geniuses

Buckminster Fuller, the late New Age architect, inventor and philosopher, whose ideas are much admired by New Agers everywhere, wrote that babies born today are natural geniuses but that their family and social environment quickly ruins them: "Every child is born a genius," said Fuller, "and then becomes de-geniused very rapidly by unfavorable circumstances and by the frustration of all the extraordinary built-in capabilities.[17] The New Age view is that parents who train their children to believe in Christian principles and ethics, patriotism and other such values are doing their children irreparable harm.

World Goodwill, a large New Age organization spun off by the Lucis Trust to better promote world unity, has expressed complete agreement with Fuller. Its proposal is that the presently negative family and social environments be changed so that success can be assured for the emerging New Age society. Then kids can reach their destined potential:

We must extend our vision and provide them (children) with an environment uplifting to their emotional, mental, and spiritual natures. In some cases this will mean limiting the availability of certain aspects of twentieth century living to our

35

children . . . so that all children will be allowed to make their individual contribution to the whole.[18]

Read again the above quote by World Goodwill officials to make sure you get the gist of what this occultic New Age organization is really saying. You will discover that the hidden meaning is this:

1. Children will be raised as *New Agers*.

2. They will be restricted from being taught to respect and honor "outmoded" Christian ethics and traditions (what World Goodwill calls "limiting the availability of certain aspects of twentieth century living").

3. Children must contribute to "the whole," rather than serve the One God or the One True Faith of Christianity.

New Age Communes Set Up

To accomplish these objectives, it may be necessary, the New Age leadership stresses, to actually set up New Age communes like the ones Alder has intricately described. Indeed, the New Age's World Goodwill has extolled the values of "the communal arrangement."[19]

Thus, we find a proliferation of New Age live-in communes and communities (see my book, *New Age Cults and Religions*). The Findhorn Community in Scotland; Paolo Soleri's Aerosanti Community in Arizona; Lindisfarne Community in Long Island, New York; and Auroville and the many Ashram communities devoted to the gurus in India are examples.

The building of numerous self-contained New Age communities—"Heavenly Cities"—by the Maharishi Mahesh Yogi is another example. Yogi, the guru for the Beatles and the Beach Boys, and the person who brought Hindu religious rituals, visualization and meditation to the United States, deceptively calling it Vedic Science and Transcendental Meditation (TM), has announced plans to build a string of lavish New Age Communities around the world. In these spiritual Shangri-La's, states Yogi, people will live in "heavenly bliss." And, the Guru says, through the combined mind powers generated by the man-gods in these communities, "heaven on earth" will be realized. Indeed, Yogi's development company is named Heaven on Earth Development Corporation.[20]

His plans are not entirely pipe dreams. In suburban Austin, Texas and near some other cities, Yogi has bought up large tracts of valuable land. His architects are busy with blueprints and other work, and a number of influential bankers and developers have signed on to help the Maharishi complete his New Age vision of Heaven on Earth through interlinking communities of believers.

However, impressive though the many current projects may be, the New Age leadership's eventual goal is far more grandiose. A handful of isolated communities and communes cannot succeed fast enough in overthrowing the last bastions of Christianity and decency to please Satan. *So, the New Age now seeks to convert and transform the entire existing world into a succession of networking New Age Communities.* If this audacious new goal is successful, they reason, the only ones who will have to go and live in communes (actually prisons and concentration camps) will be the Christians! Spiritually inferior Christian parents and kids, unfit to live in general society, will be re-educated and deprogramed after resettlement, say New Age planners.

So, the push is now on for the New Age Community to be established right where you and I now live. Every village, town, and city and every subdivision and borough shall become a New Age Community. Every home shall as well. For in Community alone, the New Age preaches, is salvation.

In Community Lies Salvation

Vladimir Lenin, the founder of Soviet communism, had his "dictatorship of the proletariat," a theory by which the *state* rules with an iron fist. Parents could be arrested and sent to Gulag prison camps and their children turned over to the state. Entire families could be herded together into industrial and agricultural communes where communist cells could minutely dictate family policy, and severely limit parental authority.

In the communist view, families are bourgeois holdovers to be eliminated, and children are the property of the state. Lenin, Stalin, and others in the Kremlin elite called their theory the *collectivization* of society. Mao Tse Tung in China and Pol Pot in Cambodia also believed in and enforced collectivization.

Now come the New Agers introducing this very same doctrine in shiny new wrappings. Old wine in new bottles. No longer are parents in charge of their children, say the

New Age plotters, and no longer does "God" care about the individual family or the individual child. Collectivization is the new principle. Even *individual salvation*—regeneration of the heart though the power of Jesus—is to be superseded by the superiority of the group, the collective, the *Community*:

> *We now enter a period wherein the goal of*
> *individual salvation is no longer appropriate. Our*
> *guidance calls for a collective transformation.*[21]

M. Scott Peck, the New Age author who delights in being called a "Christian psychiatrist," but who journeyed to India to study under the Hindu gurus and today practices mysticism and Zen Buddhism, affirms this New Age goal of replacing both God's salvation of the individual and the traditional family with the New Age version of Community. He states the New Age position in these stark, dramatic terms:

> *In and through Community lies the salvation of the*
> *world. Nothing is more important. . . . For the*
> *human race today stands at the brink of self-*
> *annihilation. . . . I'm scared for my own skin. I'm*
> *even more scared for this skin of my children and*
> *I'm scared for your skins. I want to save your skin.*
> *I need you, and you need me, for salvation. We*
> *must come into Community with each other.*[22]

According to Peck, we will not have Community until we root out the evil in society. And *what* or *whom* is evil? Well, says Peck, those who don't believe in and promote this New Age theory of Community—*they* are the evil. In this regard, Peck approvingly mentions his hero, Swiss psychiatrist Carl Jung. "Jung ascribed human evil to the refusal to meet the Shadow," Peck explains. What we must do, then, according to Peck, is meet the "Shadow" in our own personality and embrace him (or, it!) To refuse to do so, he believes, is to be an evil person—a person imbued with "militant ignorance."[23]

Community and Kingdom Now/Dominion Theology

Peck, who has founded an organization called the Foundation for Community Encouragement to propagate his views, has views similar to the heretical Kingdom Now, Restoration, Dominion Theology, and Reconstructionist doctrines now pervasive in many Christian churches. Such doctrines are accepted by the leaders of the Catholic Church and pushed by many other misguided charismatic, evangelical, and fundamentalist Protestant leaders. According to this New Age teaching, it is up to man to set up an earthly kingdom *without Jesus Christ coming first!* The Bible tells us that at the last day, Jesus Christ will come to put things right on planet Earth. He will set up his millennial kingdom and reign for a thousand years (see Revelation 19-22). This is our blessed hope and promise.

Peck and the other Kingdom/Now Dominion theorists do not agree with the clear teachings of the Bible. *Man, collectively,* will organize and establish the Kingdom, they say. Peck and some others call this coming kingdom of man "Community." Men, they say, will group themselves together in Community units, then coalesce into ever widening communities of human beings. Finally, there will be a united human *Global Community* and the New Age kingdom will have arrived. Man will be exalted to the hilt. Then shall the New Age Christ come to reign over a kingdom which *man* collectively has already won.

In the radiant dreams of the New Age dominionists, Community replaces the Jesus revealed to us in the Bible as the only hope for man's survival.

M. Scott Peck has bought the New Age lie and now spreads it about like smelly natural fertilizer. In essence, he endorses a New World Order and calls for the dissolving of the American state.[24] Then, praising the explosion in numbers of people believing in the mystical New Age religion, he excitedly exclaims:

> *One wonders if the explosion in their numbers might represent a giant leap forward in the evolution of the human race, a leap toward not only mystical but global consciousness and world Community.*[25]

Is the Divinity of Jesus a Heresy?

The only true obstacle to unity, to "holistic" Community, decries Peck, are those misled Christians who overemphasize the divinity of Jesus! This is heresy, he declares. He scathingly criticizes "heretical" and "blasphemous" Christians who put "99.5 percent of their money on Jesus' divinity and 0.5 percent on his humanity."[26]

In *The Road Less Traveled*, M. Scott Peck writes that all humans are divine beings evolving toward godhood. In the New Age view, Jesus is just another divine man who evolved. Moreover, Peck, a believer in the unity of all religions, leaves little doubt that he despises fundamentalist—that is, Biblical Christianity.

In yet another book, *A Different Drum: Community and Peacemaking,* Peck relates that he once spent a weekend with a Christian couple who began every sentence with "the Lord did this" or "the Lord did that." "When I finally escaped from them at the end of the weekend," he writes, "if I had to hear 'the Lord did this' one more time I would have puked."[27]

M. Scott Peck, a man who has fully embraced the New Age lie, may indeed have puked, but God will bless those who humble themselves before Him and give Him credit and thanksgiving for all things.

Modern Psychology Endorses Community

Peck is at least accurate in one thing he says. He glorifies modern psychology for its role in abolishing the old ideas of family, national cohesiveness, and loyalty and for promoting the concept of Community. "The whole thrust of modern psychology," he writes, "is to move the family more in the direction of Community. The average family has a long way to go in that direction. But we are moving."[28]

Most of today's psychologists and psychiatrists agree with Peck. This is why psychology has become the key entry point into the New Age for many millions of people who no longer look to the Bible as our guide for daily living. As a result, families are divided and parental roles are in shambles. Then, after *causing* the break-up of the family, such New Age psychologists as Carl Rogers can trumpet the sad news that "Marriage and the nuclear family constitute a failing way of life."[29]

First, they endeavor and often succeed in destroying our Christian, God-ordained families, then they move in to fill up the void with their New Age version of family, which is, of course, Community.

It is a horrendous thing that many who call themselves "Christian" psychologists are knowingly or unknowingly aiding this New Age cause by putting psychology first over the Bible. Counselors who do not believe the Bible is the single, reliable and authoritative guide to daily living should be ashamed to call themselves "Christian" psychologists.

Community: The New Age-Communist Connection

The anti-family, anti-America biases of the New Age are becoming more and more transparent. Also becoming transparent, as we have observed, is the New Age-Communist connection. It is, in fact, quite natural that the New Age religion and World Communism should find common ground. After all, both were devised by the same hellish author. Both exalt man directly and Lucifer indirectly. Both are lies.

It should not amaze us then that in the 14½ hour made-for-TV movie *Amerika*, which depicted a Soviet takeover and occupation of the United States, the pro-Soviet character

"Milford" delivered an eloquent speech which embodied this bold assertion:

> *We are the voice of the New generation. We are the voice of the New people. The destructive ways of the past are gone. We will replace them with our vision of the future. The past will lead us to the New Age. There have been those who have tried to stop the New Age. They are the corrupt reminder of the past. They have tried to confuse us with the idea that old America was a good country. We know that lie. History teaches us that lie. We are grateful to our Soviet brother who saved the world from destruction and we can now join him in a World of Socialist Brotherhood. Everyone will go to school. Everyone will have a job. Everyone will be equal. No one will exploit or be exploited. And all those who oppose this wonderful vision will be crushed.[30]*

In the Soviet model a Community does not have to be a rural commune, an isolated or separate hamlet, or a separated people inside a walled city. A Community is, instead, the coming together of the people within any geographical area—even the whole world—to accomplish commonly agreed upon communist objectives. The New Age Community also has agreed upon objectives. For example, it is commonly agreed that parents cannot be allowed to teach their children that the Bible is inerrant. Nor can they be permitted to instruct their children the "pernicious, separatist" doctrine that Jesus is *the* way, *the* truth, *the* life. The Community must set up sanctions to prevent this.

The New Age leadership insists that the loving, peaceful citizens grouped as One in each Community must come down hard on Christian parents and limit their authority over their children. If necessary, their children will be taken away from the Christian parents and raised by the Community.

Community is the Body of Satan

In reality, "Community" is just another synonym for "Satan." It is the world culture and the seeds which grow to become the *body of Satan*, whereas the Church is the body of Christ. Furthermore, Satan's Community—his unholy spirit—can be discovered in a number of locales. Community is wherever one finds Satan's influence. As ardent New Age theologian David Spangler has written:

> *Community . . . is the seedbed of culture . . . the seedbed where seeds are nourished. A Community is not necessarily a group of people living separate from the rest of society. . . . Community can take many forms. A Community can be a neighborhood within a city. It can be co-workers within a corporation or industry. It can be a school or members of an association. It can be a family. It can be two people: the couple is Community. The spirit of Community can even live in just one person. . . . My invisible spirit friend John has often commented that the soul is a Community.[31]*

In short, using our knowledge of the New Age, we can briefly but most accurately define Community this way: *Community is the explicit presence of Satan. Community is evidenced by Satanic ownership and influence.*

In the New Age view, the family is the whole Community. But not so in the Christian worldview. The whole purpose of the Christian family is to bring its members into a harmonious relationship under the authority and Lordship of Jesus Christ. In essence, the purpose of the family is to worship the one true God. But, as one New Age child care expert has observed, the purpose of the New Age Community family is distinctively different: "The purpose of family," this New Age specialist writes, "is to protect the divinity in each of its members."[32] In other words, the New Age family exists to become its own God, rather than to serve the God of the Bible.

"Christian" Leaders Join the New Age Community Bandwagon

A number of misguided, so-called "Christian" leaders have rallied around the "Community" banner of the New Age. The New Age drive to communize kids and separate them from parents is also encouraged by Planned Parenthood, the National Committee for Prevention of Child Abuse, and similar groups.

Robert Runcie, who as the Archbishop of Canterbury was until recently the spiritual and administrative leader of the Church of England, has, like other New Age leaders, called for an end to the traditional Christian doctrine of *personal salvation.* "We must," he has stated, "reject such a privatization of religion which results in . . . personal salvation."[33]

Meanwhile, the Rev. W. Franklin Richardson, a member of the Central Committee of the World Council of Churches (note that the Soviet Communist Party also has its "Central Committee") has compared the concept of Community, which he approves, to that of the "global village:"

> *The World Council of Churches . . . is similar to the United Nations of the Church. . . . I think that the future of the world is that we are becoming . . . the "global village." . . . We are in one world, one Community. . . . The church is going home to aid the world in understanding that and the United States is going to have to come to grips with that.*[34]

The federal government, as well as many national child welfare organizations, is also backing the New Age campaign to destroy the family unit, eradicate parental authority and install despotic rule by the "Community." One very prominent example is the work of the well-known National Committee for the Prevention of Child Abuse (NCPCA). In a resource packet for Christian religious leaders developed by the NCPCA, the authors refuse to identify God as "Our Father." They go on to reject Biblical truths and attempt to subvert readers by inserting in the resources packet information promoting the New Age philosophy of Community. Even to the extent of blasphemously claiming that "Christ" is simply a "loving Community."

> *To children, the hope of New Life must come*
> *through a loving Community—the personification of*
> *the Risen Christ.*[35]

The NCPCA material favorably notes that "the traditional image of the family" is changing. Community, they suggest, is on the ascendance while the traditional family ordained by God is on the way out. As the young grow into adulthood and are separated from their parents, say the authors, they must seek and find a new "family of choice."[36] This is the same New Age propaganda line being pushed by many psychologists today as well as by such groups as the Adult Children of Alcoholics organizations.

The most horrible aspect of the NCPCA propaganda is that the organization redefines the Christian "church." No longer is the church composed of individuals who have accepted Jesus as Lord and Savior and who obey His commandments and cherish His Word in their hearts. Instead, according to the NCPCA, the church is simply the whole of society. The church is, in effect, *Community*.[37]

In the near future, look for this disingenuous concept to receive greater emphasis. Satan no doubt finds great pleasure in labeling the church as the equivalent of the New Age's Community, and he likewise mockingly delights in redefining Christ Himself as Community.

The New Age as Big Brother

Our good friend, able Christian researcher and writer Mary Pride (*All the Way Home, The Child Abuse Industry, Unholy Sacrifices of the New Age*, and other books), was instrumental in bringing to my attention some of the abuses of the National Committee for Prevention of Child Abuse as well as the New Age policies of other federal agencies. In a recent letter, she eloquently stated the horrific proportions of this New Age takeover of governmental child "watchdog" agencies:

When you realize, as I have found out through my research, that the (state and local) Family Services/ Health and Human Services departments all around this country are loaded with New Agers, witchcraft-oriented feminists, and the like, it becomes truly alarming.

These people wield coercive government authority. They can remove your children from your house and put them into "their" houses. Christians are being shut out of foster care due to anti-spanking and pro-secular psychology laws now passed or being passed around the country. At the same time, homosexuals, rabid feminists, and so on—many of whom are New Agers—are being recruited or are pressing for the right to be foster parents.

Along with this is the push for in-home visits by government agents to determine whether a family should be allowed to continue to raise its own children. They plan to start with first-time parents, who will be insecure and less likely to understand the ramifications of the New Age child-rearing methods. The New Age methods, parents will be told, are the only right way to raise children.

The government is positioning itself as the prophet of an "orthodox" (New Age) way to raise kids— and calling all other ways child abuse. At the same time New Agers are taking over these government agencies.

This is more than ravaging our children. . . . They are actually trying to STEAL them from us!

Texe, I am praying that you will be able to share this information with the public in your new book. You are in the best position of any of us to blow the whistle on these guys before it gets too late. People NEED TO KNOW.

PART III

The Bold New Age Claim: Christian Parents Are Ignorant, Insane, Unstable, Unfit

If the world hate you, ye know that it hated me before it hated you. If ye were of the world, the world would love its own; but because ye are not of the world, therefore the world hateth you.
John 15:18-19

Remember the Word that I said unto you, The servant is not greater than his Lord. If they have persecuted me, they will also persecute you.
John 15:20

The fundamentalist Christians are the worst Christians. They are the most fanatic people. They believe that Christianity is the only religion. . . . These are primitive ideas.
Bhagwan Rajneesh

It can no longer be accepted that parents have sole authority over their children.
World Goodwill

Get ready for a tidal wave of persecution and revulsion against Christian parents. I'm talking about parents who know and love Jesus Christ, honor His Word, and bring up their children in the admonition of the Lord. If you fall into this despised category, the world hates you. And the New Age, as the world's chosen end-time religion, is paving the way for your children to be taken from your custody. After all, according to New Age doctrine and teachings, you are a threat to your children's well being. You are a member of a "fundamentalist cult."

Now keep in mind that the New Age has no argument with parents who are *ecumenical Christians*—"Christians" who believe that all paths lead to God and that unity comes before doctrine. Such believers will find much in common with New Agers. *Cosmic Christians*, too, are celebrated as brethren by New Age teachers. Cosmic Christians are those who enjoy being called Christians but who deny John 1— the Truth that Jesus Christ, the Word, was and is God of the universe. No, the New Age aims its hatred and venom only at one small group of Christians—Biblical Christian fundamentalist parents.

I have documented the evidence that Satan wants our children. Now, we will examine a key way in which they hope to achieve this despicable goal—the New Age plot to discredit and destroy the effectiveness and reputation of Christian parents. Bluntly stated, New Age psychologists, educators, sociologists and other family "experts" are making this bold claim: *Christian parents are ignorant, insane, unstable, unfit.*

Alice Bailey, writing as the mouthpiece of her demon guide, Djwhal Khul, the Tibetan Master, is one of the New Age elitists who has spearheaded the drive to capture our kids by undermining parental control. Her organization, World Goodwill, affiliated with the Lucis Trust, detailed some of its in-depth agenda in a guide called *The World's Most Precious Resource: Its Children.*[1] With its benign title, one would think this is a harmless and beneficial guide for parents and others concerned about children. Regrettably, this isn't the case.

In the distorted New Age view, children are a precious resource because they are considered to be most vulnerable and soft targets for New Age propaganda and indoctrination. Children are curious, questioning, tentative, tender, sensitive and innocent. They *want* to believe adults. They are like lambs to the slaughter for the determined and disciplined New Age teacher and leader. Even worse and much more grievous is the situation in which children are being raised by parents who are hardcore New Age occultists.

The New Age Lie: Family Breakdown Has a Silver Lining

In her New Age report on children, Alice Bailey cleverly weaves together the reasoning behind the decades-long assault on youth. First, she points to the breakdown of society, the church and the family, suggesting that this breakdown has a silver lining because *it creates unique opportunities for fulfillment of the New Age Plan:*

> *It is said that prior to all new growth . . . there is ever a breaking down of the old structures.*

Institutions and belief systems that have been formulated throughout the past centuries are . . . no longer adequate to meet the needs of a changing planet.

Such conditions lead us to the present problem and the resultant opportunity—an opportunity to provide . . . children with the environment which their sensitivity demands.[2]

To take advantage of this opportunity, Bailey offers a number of suggestions. First, noting the youth rebellion against authority and the increasing tendency of teens to commit violence and crimes, she recommends a new attitude be adopted—an attitude of permissiveness:

An interesting experiment was taken . . . by a man named Homer Lane. He worked with children who had committed crimes . . . He viewed children from a different perspective when he heard the record of the evil the children had committed, instead of pitying them as poor little sinners, he could admire them as stout-hearted little ruffians . . . He was able to see in those crimes evidence of qualities admirable in themselves and, when differently expressed, recognizable.[3]

A second guideline of Bailey's is that New Agers should encourage the idea that traditional parents (fundamentalist Christians, for example) are irreparably harming their children and, therefore, society must establish new ways of bringing up children:

Today the average child is, for the first five or six years of life, the victim of his parents' ignorance or selfishness . . . The damage done to children . . . is often irremediable and is responsible for much of the pain and suffering in later life.[4]

As Bailey's statement makes clear, Satan's New Age strategy is to label all fundamentalists—that is, Biblical Christians—as ignorant and selfish. They are too strict, set too many rules, put "guilt trips" on kids and try to enforce their "archaic" Biblical laws. All of this, the claim goes, damages children's minds and leads to lifelong mental pain and suffering. This is the same lie the leaders of Fundamentalists Anonymous and other ungodly groups feed to TV masses on such TV programs as *The Phil Donahue Show* and *The Geraldo Show.*

From the highest levels in the New Age the directive has gone out to the workers in the field: brand Christian fundamentalist parents as paranoid, stupid, ignorant, uncouth, divisive, evil, unloving, spiritually inferior beings. Hindu guru Bhagwan Rajneesh preached, "The fundamentalist Christians are the worst Christians. They are the most fanatic people. They believe that Christianity is the only religion. . . . These are very primitive ideas."[5]

New Age psychologist and occult author Robert Anton Wilson has also strongly denounced brave and faithful Christians who stand up for Jesus. "To me," Wilson snapped to an interviewer, "fundamentalism . . . is conducive to stupidity and interferes with the proper functioning of intelligence, creativity, joy and having a good time."[6]

In one of her many bestselling books, Ruth Montgomery, often described as the "Herald of the New Age," railed against those Christians who refuse to unify with the New Age, scathingly declaring, "So many are ignorant, with closed minds and little education, that they fail to realize the close relationship between the ancient Eastern religions and that which Christ brought to the world."[7]

Children's Needs to be Met Outside the Home

Because the traditional parents—"ignorant and spiritually unreliable"—cannot be entrusted with their children and because of other social forces, say New Age leaders, children's needs will have to be met *outside of the home.* Using this rationale, the New Age leaders are pushing for government-run and controlled daycare facilities. They are also vigorously promoting the establishment of New Age communes and communities. In such a community, the reasoning goes, working parents and also parents who are too ignorant to bring up their children according to the "needs of the New Age," can turn their kids over to trained "experts." Bailey explains it this way:

> *It seems apparent that the future will increasingly see the needs of children, from a very young age, being met outside the home. . . . With such a situation it seems apparent that state, national, and global agencies should be in the forefront of the movement towards providing quality childcare facilities.*[8]

The thrust of the New Age Plan is to take all authority away from parents—especially Christian parents—and place it in the hands of the New Age experts. Such experts include daycare workers and teachers trained to lead kids in guided mental imagery exercises, earth worship, witchcraft and Native American Indian rituals, and other New Age atrocities. Naturally, the New Age psychologists, psychiatrists, and other mental health "professionals" will also play an important part in raising our kids, as will the holistic health practitioners, shamans, and technicians.

The United Nations Assists the New Age

An ingenious vehicle invented to aid in the fulfillment of the New Age goal is the United Nations-sponsored *Declaration of the Rights of the Child*. This declaration, drafted formally by UNICEF and signed by the representatives of almost every nation on earth, is designed to strip away parents' rights, yet it seems on the surface to be harmlessly devoted to insuring children's rights: a perfect example of New Age doublespeak.

Perhaps the most odious provision of the UN's *Declaration of the Rights of the Child* is Principle 10:

> *The child shall be protected from practices which may foster racial, religious and any other form of discrimination. He shall be brought up in a spirit of understanding, tolerance, friendship among peoples, peace and universal brotherhood and in full consciousness that his energy and talents should be devoted to the service of his fellow men.*[9]

The implications of the wording in Principle 10 of the UN's *Declaration of the Rights of the Child* are staggering. The child cannot be brought up in the Christian faith since the Christian doctrine that Jesus is the only way to salvation is a form of discrimination. Preaching the gospel is out

57

since to do so would be to foster a belief in the exclusive nature of Christianity. Finally, in this principle, we have the nations of the world asserting that the child must be instructed that "his energy and talents should be devoted to the service of his fellow men" rather than to God.

This is in marked contrast to the Bible's unarguable teaching that we are to love God and serve Him first and foremost. Then and only then are we to serve our fellow man and devote ourselves in service to humanity.

Children Will Not be Raised to Serve Christ Jesus

The New Age game plan is to deify—makes gods of—humanity. Obviously, it is first necessary to destroy the child's faith in the one true God, the true Christ, Jesus, our Lord and Savior. And to do this, the authority and ability of Christian parents to raise their child in the admonition of the Lord must be severely limited and curtailed. If possible, it is to be completely severed. In extreme cases, children may either have to be removed from the home entirely, or placed in the custodial care of New Age childcare authorities and experts.

Of course, this will be justified as defending the children's right to a safe, secure future in New Age Society. As a *Commentary* of World Goodwill, the New Age organization jointly headquartered in the United States, London, and Geneva craftily reasons:

> *There exists today the growing recognition that some children cannot always be thought safe and in*

the best care merely by the fact that they are living with their parents. It can no longer be accepted that parents have sole authority over their children. The situation is so out of control that we, as a global society, must take action towards the restoration of true liberty in the home as well as in society at large.[10]

It is true that parents have no right to mentally, physically or sexually abuse their children. All Christians can agree on this. God even tells us not to provoke our children to anger. The true Christian home is a model of gentleness and consideration, a sanctuary of firm discipline wisely mixed with love and tenderness. But this isn't sufficient for New Age leaders. They also insist that children not be taught the basics of Christian faith. The New Age leadership claims that this constitutes child abuse. It is, they say, mental and spiritual torture brought about by parental ignorance.

Increasingly, the world is falling for the New Age lies. The Christian parent who believes in Jesus and his Word is being labeled and characterized as an unfit parent, an unstable member of the "Fundamentalist Cult." If the New Age elite has its way, the government will someday rule that it is totally unacceptable for parents to teach true Biblical Christianity to their children. If that despicable day ever dawns, the devil will have achieved his goal of undermining America. Alice Bailey, who has resolutely trumpeted, "A new form of family united must inevitably come into existence," will have gotten her way. Our kids will become spiritual cannon fodder for Satan's ravenously awaiting legions of demons.

Honor Your Child as "God"

The New Age has come up with a diabolical justification for their plan to separate children from their Christian parents. After first teaching youth to defy and despise parental authority and after successfully causing society to unfairly brand and label Christian parents mentally unfit and spiritually ignorant, the crowning blow will be a New Age claim that children today are spiritually superior to their parents. Children are to be honored as gods.

The startling and ingenious plan of the New Age is to portray our children as reincarnated, spiritually advanced entities. Our kids, the New Age story goes, are reincarnated Ascended Masters full of divine human potential. As higher order beings, the reasoning goes, these "gods-in-becoming" cannot be allowed to be held back from achieving their full human potential by mentally unfit and spiritually ignorant parents. It will be necessary for the state to step in and take control of, protect, and guide our kids' development. The shocking plan, then, calls for our children's "divine potential" to be realized by their "global family." They must become wards of the state. Rights of parents must give way to the rights of the child to become a god!

The speeches and writings of the New Age elite could not be more transparent. Our kids are to be honored as gods and be spiritually and mentally—in extreme cases, physically—separated from parents. To condition society for this upcoming, dramatic change in the family unit, the New Age propagandists are hard at work. Alice Bailey capsulized this bizarre New Age doctrine when she stated, "the children who are coming into incarnation are necessarily on the verge of soul consciousness." Therefore, said Bailey, "we, as a global community, will soon come to this decision and place our children at the top of our list of priorities."[11]

Continuing, Bailey argued that "todays children are different . . . their intelligence is a product of the evolutionary tide." As evolving divine beings, Bailey writes, our children are accelerating the present breakdown in society—a trend which she obviously found highly encouraging.[12]

Swami Muktananda, the Hindu guru responsible for spiritually mentoring and introducing a large number of current New Age leaders to their twisted religious beliefs, taught them that children are God; therefore, "You should honor them as God."[13]

New Age Education to be the Norm For Our Kids

Robert Muller, former Assistant Secretary General of the United Nations and a high-level mover and shaker in the New Age, has stated that the proper instruction of young people is an instrumental part of the New Age agenda, an agenda that must be "resolved at all costs" if the New Age soul of man is to achieve the uttermost fulfillment of its powers and destiny.[14]

Muller, the "Father of New Age Global Education," preached that "Global education must prepare our children for the coming of an interdependent, safe, prosperous, friendly, loving planetary age."[15] A significant feature of Muller's Global Education Curriculum for our children would be the teaching of religion. But not the *Christian* religion! Heavens, no! What Muller has in mind is a blended ecumenical religion of all faiths—Hindu, Buddhist, Christian, and so forth.[16] Muller further believes that children should be taught that the United Nations is the "body of Christ" and he recommends a new Bible should be written to foster New Age ideas, which he refers to as "the ecumenical teachings of the Christ," and as "a new morality and ethics."[17]

In Muller's influential book, *New Genesis: Shaping a Global Spirituality,* he emphasizes that, as evolving deities, our children must be raised to appreciate their role as divine beings. For this role to be realized and for a Golden Age to transpire, the world's major religions must "recognize the *unity* of their objectives in the diversity of their *cults*." Moreover, such concepts as "My religion, right or wrong" and "My nation, right or wrong" must be abandoned in the planetary age.[18]

Virginia Essene, in *New Teachings for an Awakened Humanity,* supposedly given to her by her spirit guide who identified himself as "Christ," also adds her clout to the New Age cry for a new era of parenting. "Beginning in the last decade," her "Christ" is quoted as saying, reincarnated "children with old souls came with an eagerness to express God's love, grow in light and understanding, and to populate the planet preparatory for the thousand years of peace."

Many will be masters of truth, heralds of this upcoming Golden Age, who need your unique nurturing.[19]

Essene's "Christ" wants society to raise little "positive thinkers." He (or it) stresses that "the fewer false beliefs you fill a child with the less cleansing she/he will have to do later.[20]   What false beliefs is this New Age "Christ" concerned about? Well, for one he wants children to be taught that God is love only, that "God does not punish." (Thus, there is no hell, no judgement, in clear contrast to Jesus' teachings.)[21]   Second, this lying "Christ" presents the "new gospel" of the Golden Age, a gospel requiring people only to meditate and seek guidance from the spirit world, "the fourth dimension of consciousness." You cannot serve "God" in this New Age, this false "Christ" teaches, by holding on to "obsolete" Christian beliefs contained in the Bible:

> *My brothers and sisters, it is not appropriate that you deny this new spiritual information that I bring because of the Bible ... If you cleave only to the exact wording of the holy book which was released as a guide for past times ... you will not be growing in the way God wishes. Your interpretation of all holy books must be expanded to recognize the higher vibrations now being transmitted ... Some insist the Bible is a final work ... To these ideas I say a resounding NO![22]*

Childhood's End

In his classic novel of some years ago, *Childhood's End*, New Age science fiction writer Arthur Clarke presented a dark picture of what I believe is chillingly reminiscent of the brave new world the New Age wants for us and our children.

In his novel, Clarke paints scary scenes of planet Earth on the very threshold of unparalleled world war and nuclear catastrophe. Suddenly, enormous spaceships carrying "Overlords" appear over the major capitols of the world and, though unseen, begin issuing dire and grave warnings to mankind. They back up their demands with effective demonstrations of great power. Purged of resistance, the human leaders of earth give in and begin to follow the instructions they receive from these powerful, unseen "Overlords" out in space.

Thus, through man's own efforts, the work of the Overlords begins in earnest. Soon, a new race of "wonder children" are created who represent the next step in evolution for humanity. . . . These children are like gods. They wield vast, miraculous psychic powers, yet they are slaves, for each is merely a single cell in the Overmind of the Universe.

The New Age plot to conquer our children and transform them into New Age "godlings" could have well been lifted right off the pages of this fascinating but evil Arthur Clarke science fiction novel. The same elements exist—a "Hierarchy" of Overlords, led by the Prince of the Power of the Air (Satan, see Eph. 2:2), operate behind the scenes. These evil entities are motivating the leaders of earth to mold their vulnerable and malleable children into monstrous New Age creations held in bondage by a demon Overmind, an Overmind named Lucifer.

PART IV

They Want Our Children

*And he took a child, and set him in the midst of
them: and when he had taken him in his arms, he
said unto them. Whosoever shall receive one of
such children in my name, receiveth me . . .*
                                        Mark 9:36-37

*Thus, tenderly, Ascended Lady Master Nada
sponsors the world's children, individual by
individual . . . and she has legions of angels who
personally attend the little ones and the youth.*
                              Elizabeth Clare Prophet
                              Lord of the Seven Rays

Satan wants our children. He wants them for his evil
kingdom. He wants them so God, whom he hates with
unbridled passion, can't have them. And, to achieve his
Secret Plan to capture and destroy our kids, he has raised
up an ever growing horde, or congregation, of New Age
believers. Inspired by their demon spirit guides, the leaders
of this New Age rebellion against God have made the
possession of our kid's souls one of their top priorities.

Children's Minds Targeted

Top New Age guru David Spangler, formerly spokesperson for Scotland's Findhorn Community and now associate of the Cathedral of St. John the Divine in New York, emphasizes the depth and extent of the New Age commitment when, in simple but menacing terms, he recently stated, "The New Age *is* our children."

Spangler stresses that *everything* New Age leaders and followers are doing is designed, ultimately, with children in mind. New Agers must insure that children become integrated into the New Age, he says. Moreover, New Agers must work to change the earth so that children can be "whole, healthy and safe" and "grow and prosper."[1]

"There are three images to help us define the New Age," writes Spangler, "*children, earth*, and the *change of mind* that responds to the crises and opportunities of our time."[2]

When Spangler speaks of the *change of mind* needed to bring in the New Age, you should understand that he is referring to the New Age insistence that Christianity must turn away from its "stubborn" belief that Jesus is the only way and come into unity with all other world religions and cults. This is the most wicked and most persistent of New Age tenets. It is being taught to our children in movies, TV, books, comic books, and by many school teachers. Wherever our children turn they are hearing the insidious New Age refrain of how evil Christians are for wishing to remain separate from the other religious groups.

Elizabeth Clare Prophet, head of the New Age's Church Universal and Triumphant and a big promoter of the unholy

Montessori Schools for children, is yet another of the many New Age leaders who are seeking to change our children's minds. Her aim is to picture Christians as just a group of evil separatists. This is why, in her book, *Lord of the Seven Rays*, through a spirit named Lord Lanto, Prophet exclaims:

> *Can you not see how these serpents* (i.e. fundamentalist Christians!) *have contrived to be karma-dodgers and to place upon the Children of the Light worldwide ... their own guilt, their own self-condemnation, their own fear of death and hell?*[3]

According to Prophet, two powerful spirit guides especially have a keen interest in children. The first is a "Lady Master Nada" who supposedly assists the "New Age Hierarch, Count St. Germaine," in the spirit realm:

> *Assisting St. Germaine in his "great gathering of the elect" who will serve with him in the cause of world freedom is beloved Nada .... This Ascended Lady Master also serves on the Karmic Board.*[4]

"On Atlantis" (the fabled island which many New Agers claim really existed), Prophet writes, "Nada served as a priestess in the Temple of Love."[5]

Spirit Guide to Lead Children

Elizabeth Clare Prophet also says that spirit guide Lady Master Nada is in charge of the gift of tongues--both "diverse kinds of tongues and the interpretation of tongues" on planet earth. She was, adds Prophet, the etheric model for America's Statute of Liberty, and so she can be addressed as "The Goddess of Liberty."[6] But in this age, her main task is to oversee and supervise the Plan with regard to children:

> *Thus, tenderly, Nada sponsors the world's children, individual by individual . . . and she has legions of angels who personally attend the little ones and the youth.*[7]

> *Nada is especially concerned that incoming souls receive the necessary spiritual, practical, academic education and that parents need to give their children . . . discipleship under the Cosmic Christ.*[8]

Below, according to Prophet, is how spirit/guide and Ascended Lady Master Nada--supposedly speaking in her own voice--answered the prayer of one little girl:

> *I remember many years ago when a little girl who did not even know of the existence of the Masters of Wisdom prayed to God and said, "O Father, if thou hast any servant upon this earth or anywhere in the universe that will love me and help me, thou dost not need to come thyself, but send them and I will receive them as thyself."*

> *And when she prayed thusly, I was sent. And I appeared to her at first only as in a dream. She saw me surrounded with roses, and having a parochial background she fancied that I was Mother Mary. And so, in one of her dreams Mother Mary came also with me, and then she (the little girl) was confused and said, "Oh, you have a sister."*[9]

Is Nada the Harlot of Mystery Babylon?

Lady Master Nada is nothing more than a New Age representation of the Mother Goddess of Babylon—the harlot of Revelation 17. Whether she exists as a demon spirit or as a figment of Elizabeth Clare Prophet's obviously fertile imagination is quite irrelevant. Whichever is the case, Prophet and others use this image of the Great Mother, the Goddess, to arouse and incite the passions of their followers and to teach them New Age doctrines.

Mother Mary and the New Age Rosary

References to Mary, Jesus' mother, are also common in the New Age ministry of Elizabeth Clare Prophet. Indeed, Prophet claims that Mary came to her in a vision and gave her an entire book of instructions:

> *I was walking, fairly skipping along the side-walk . . . praying and talking to God in joyous realization of . . . the Ascended Masters. . . . All of a sudden I looked up and there she was! I was face to face with the Blessed Mother . . . the beautiful Mary, a being of great light. A charge of light and indescribable joy passed through my body.[10]*

Prophet's vision is recounted in a 345-page book entitled *My Soul Doth Magnify the Lord*, touted as "Mother Mary's New Age teachings and rosary with a challenge to Christendom."[11] According to Prophet, this demon spirit, who comes to trick and deceive as the Mary of the Bible, claims to be the great I Am. Prophet's "Mother Mary" states that before Abraham was, *she (or it!) was*.[12] Blasphemously posing as "the bride of the Holy Spirit" and pretending to be "Queen of the Universe," the New Age "Mary" solemnly declares war against the cancerous Christians who oppose New Age unity:

> *He that is not for me--the Cosmos that I am--is against me. . . . Therefore, we mobilize to exorcise the cancer of self-apartness that is eating away at the Body of God.*[13]

Is the New Age "Mary" a Member of the Holy Trinity?

She is one of the Ascended Masters, explains Elizabeth Clare Prophet of the false Mother Mary who appeared to her, "who has reunited with the Trinity."[14] Prophet states also that this Mary is the same Mother Goddess the Hindus call by Kundalini, Kali and other divine names:

> *The Hindus have meditated upon Mother and called Her the Goddess Kundalini, describing Her as the white light, or the coiled serpent. . . . The Hindus have (also) called Her the Divine Shakti--the Great Counterpart, the Conscious Force of the Trinity.*[15]

The spirit known to her as "Mother Mary" gave Prophet a brand new rosary for the Age of Aquarius, the New Age. She stipulates that this rosary is to be used by the whole world. Catholics and non-Catholics alike. Speaking in glowing terms about the Lords of Karma in the spirit world and of Count St. Germaine, "Mary" praises Buddha as well as her "son," Jesus. But, exalting *herself* above them all she encourages people everywhere to seek "Divine Selfhood through the adoration of the Mother flame."[16]

"Claim your divinity," she implores readers.[17]

The New Age "Mary" and the Children

This "Mother Mary" obviously is clued in on the Plan by her hellish master from the pit. She gave Prophet special instructions and teachings to pass on to parents and others about children and the New Age, instructions that she said are the work of "Lord Buddha:"

> *Mothers, teach it to your children. Fathers, speak it to your sons and daughters. . . . I have seen how little children are receptive to this truth.*
>
> *And so at the request of the Lord Buddha, the Lord of the World, a program has been initiated for the incoming souls . . . until the day when. . .they can tie into the God within, until the age of reason when they can choose the godly way on their own.[18]*

This demonic being evidently well understands the Biblical principle in Proverbs 22:6, "Train up a child in the way he should go: and when he is old, he will not depart from it." Her instruction to New Agers is to reach kids early, *before* they reach the age of reason, so that they can grow up and later take part in the "Plan:"

> *For up to the age of seven, Mary stresses, there is great opportunity of sealing them in the fires of*

71

Christ. Whatever is impressed upon the clay of consciousness during the period of formation and the first seven years is most important.[19]

What the Bible Says About "Mary" and Other Spirits

Catholics are the principal targets of the New Agers now bringing the "New Gospel of Mother Mary." But there are also today a large number of protestants attracted to the many apparitions of Mary now appearing and spreading a New Age gospel. Mary, as the saintly and chaste mother of Jesus, certainly is worthy of honor and reverence. But she is not the Mother of God. Though she is in heaven, Mary cannot communicate with those on earth. God's Word clearly warns us against communication with the spirits of the dead.

The Bible stresses that Jesus alone is our intercessor and mediator with the Father (I Tim. 2:5). Moreover, Deuteronomy 18:10-12 warns:

There shall not be found among you any one that maketh his son or his daughter to pass through the fire, or that useth divination, or an observer of times, or an enchanter, or a witch, Or a charmer, or a consulter with familiar spirits, or a wizard, or a necromancer. For all that do these things are an abomination unto the Lord: and because of these abominations the Lord thy God doth drive them out from before thee.

So it is clearly an abomination to the Lord for us to even attempt to speak with spirits from the dead, even with those in heaven. For further guidance from God's Word, I refer you to: Luke 16:19-31, John 8:21, I Thes. 4, I Cor. 15:35-38, and Isaiah 8:19-20 and 47. For example, we read in Isaiah 8:19-20:

> *And when they shall say unto you, Seek unto them that have familiar spirits, and unto wizards that peep, and that mutter: should not a people seek unto their God?*

Lord Maitreya, the New Age "Christ," and His Plan for Our Kids

This same Bible admonition should be heeded by those persons being sucked in by the smooth words of "Lord Maitreya." Lord Maitreya is the lying demon spirit who comes to New Age teacher Benjamin Creme as well as many other New Agers proclaiming himself to be "the Christ" and "The Great World Teacher." Like his New Age spirit counterpart, "Mother Mary," Lord Maitreya brings special instructions regarding the Plan for kids. How horrifying that Alice Bailey, head of the Lucis Trust, identifies Maitreya as the "Nourisher of the Little Ones."[20]

Just what types of teachings does this Lord Maitreya seek to impart to our kids to "nourish" their spiritual development? Bailey lists such standard New Age occultic teachings as reincarnation, evolution, self-as-divine, the return of the Ancient Mysteries, open and frequent

73

communication with Ascended Masters in the spirit world, and the oneness of all religions (except Biblical Christianity).[21]

The "Lord Maitreya" spirit supposedly visits often with Benjamin Creme of California and London's Tara Foundation. He continually expresses a keen interest in teaching our children New Age concepts. Children, in fact, are key to his Plan. Thus, Maitreya is quoted as exclaiming:

> *My Plan is that My teaching should precede my Presence and prepare My way . . . . My Plan is to save these little ones.*[22]

To aid his Plan, Creme's Maitreya encourages all to follow him and to find the divine light that resides within each person. "Find that," he says, "and know that you are gods."[23]

The New Age Lie to Our Kids—"You Are Gods"

It is entirely understandable that the New Age would seek to convince our children that they are "little gods." This, of course, is an ages old lie of Satan, first told no doubt to the angels that he persuaded to join him in his fruitless and tragic rebellion against Almighty God. Later, on earth in the Garden, he successfully cajoled and pleaded with Eve to go ahead and eat the forbidden fruit. That she could become a god was Satan's seductive lie (Gen. 2:5). Satan is perhaps craftier today, but his lies remain the same. He convinces by appealing to man's carnal and selfish nature and by puffing men and women up with flattery.

The Bible prophesied that in the last days, Satan would train his final World Ruler, the Antichrist, to use the same technique. "He will win his kingdom through flattery" (Daniel 11:21,32). What greater flattery than to tell people they are gods? Even little children—precious yes, but sometimes disobedient and in need of correction—can be seduced by such flattery.

One treacherous flattery to our kids is that they have been "chosen" to see the promised land—the coming of the New Age Kingdom. As Vera Alder states:

> *This tremendous event will take place during the lives of those who are already born. We can look upon the little child of today with awe and envy because he will live to see the greatest event of the new era—the "second coming of Christ."* [24]

When Alder and other New Agers speak of the "second coming of Christ," they do not refer to Jesus' second coming. No, their reference is to the coming of the great man-god, the World Teacher. He is often called Lord Maitreya, but also by various other names. *Whatever name he is identified by, he will not be the Jesus of the Bible.* Alder makes this point crystal clear when she describes the new occult era of scientific prowess to come after her false "Christ" takes the reigns of world power:

> *The transition from the era of mystic emotional religion into the coming era of occult or mental religion will show Christ and His words in a different light. He will at last be understood as a profoundly scientific and practical Teacher.*

> *Religions will have to be remodeled to suit growing public intelligence . . . . Occultism, mysticism, and the barriers between them will be seen to be absurd.*[25]

The Coming Governmental Control of Parenting and Childcare

Alder says, too, that other momentous changes will be required in the fast approaching New Age Kingdom. For one thing, parents will have to give up control of their kids to the social welfare people whom, she asserts, know so much better how to raise and nurture our kids. She proposes that large institutions and clinics be set up nationwide, even globally. These government institutions can be called *Healthhouses*, Alder suggests.[26] It will be mandatory for children of all ages to be checked into a healthhouse once a year, once in six months, or sooner if ordered to do so, to be subjected to a complete physical, mental, psychic and spiritual assessment.

"Experts" at the healthhouse, writes Alder, will maintain a record, file, or dossier on each child. Periodic visits to the healthhouse will continue throughout the lifetime of the child. Alder anticipates that the experts will make sure that children develop as they should spiritually as well as culturally and recreationally. Government psychological standards must be met.

This wonderful system, Alder believes, will result in a remarkable change both in the child and in society at large:

If this regular supervision is given to a person from babyhood upwards, inhibition, repressions, and bad habits of living and thinking will be largely eliminated as soon as they appear.[27]

Loyalty to Family and Country Will Have to Go

Just what "inhibitions and repressions" do Alder and her New Age colleagues have in mind? What "bad habits" of children are to be eliminated by the psychologists, human resources and social welfare "experts" of the radiant New Age society just ahead in man's future? Well, for one thing, the child's loyalty to family and to country will have to go. This is supposedly necessary, Alder explains, because:

People have been brought up with a set of taboos, ideals and ideas automatically stamped upon them. Firstly, he was coloured by the tradition and attitude of his family . . . family pride, exclusiveness, greed, possessiveness, ambition, and narrowmindedness.

Secondly, he was given into . . . a somewhat blind "patriotism" in the interests of the state.[28]

Far better, insist the New Age planners, is the idea of Unity—for example, the achievement of a One World Government and the concept that "All the world is my family." Alder complains that the child "has been firstly educated to regard himself as a member . . . of his family, then as a member of his country. He is never represented to himself as a member of a *world* humanity."[29]

What a glorious world—a "Utopia"—it will be, suggests Alder, when national patriotism and ties to family are superseded by *world citizenship*.[30] Then, she writes, the children, as world citizens, shall be *subsidized* by the *World Government*. This will bring true freedom, for "government subsidized children will do away with much of the parental possessiveness and tyranny."[31]

Outmoded Christianity Will Have to Go

Another "inhibition" or "bad habit" that New Agers plan to eliminate in our children is the "outmoded" teachings of Christianity. In her startling but popular book, *New Teachings For an Awakening Humanity*, Virginia Essene, a well-known New Age lecturer and author, includes the instructions she says she has received directly from the New Age (or Golden Age) "Christ." A number apply to parents and teachers of children.

For example, Virginia Essene's "Christ" suggests that all parents and teachers learn to say to their children something like, "Until now . . ." or "We have believed until now . . ."[32]

"This will mean surrendering the past ideas you were taught about Christianity," Essene's New Age "Christ" explains.[33]

Also, once the New Age concepts are put in place, parents must not teach a child that "we are worms in the dust and God will get us for our sins." These types of comments, Essene emphasizes, are false and limiting.[34]

Your Child is to Communicate with the Spirits

The demonic entity masquerading as the New Age Teacher, or "Christ," further proposes that children learn from sources in the unseen, spiritual dimensions:

> *It is not I, dear ones, who has created the Plan. However, it is I, and others in heaven, who have totally accepted and participated in it. Your task is the same. For the sake of the Golden Age children, you should encourage them to experience contact with what you may not see and hear yourself.*[35]

It will therefore help tremendously, the New Age "Christ" told Virginia Essene, to help your child to communicate with the spirit world, to the "wise ones beyond the veil."

"Not only are they willing to teach the little ones," this false "Christ" assures us, "They are willing—by the process of mental telepathy—to teach *you* more of the truth of this universe and your place in it."[36]

However, the help of the "wise ones" does not come, says the "Christ," except to those who use meditation to summon them and who are grateful to the spirits for their assistance: "You must be grateful for the Divine Plan that God has given humankind."[37]

Your Child Should Be Sexually Active

Another way in which the New Age seeks to poison our children's minds is by the promotion of free and illicit sex and immorality. Homosexuality and bi-sexuality are accepted, even encouraged by the New Age teacher. The unholy doctrine of reincarnation and the principle of *yin/yang* are perfect excuses and rationale for homosexuality and other forms of sexual immorality. If you are a homosexual or a lesbian in this lifetime, New Age teachers believe that it is probably because you were a person of the opposite sex in a previous incarnation or past life. The residue and influence of that past life is simply retained within your brain and consciousness.

The *yin/yang* principle, also called *unity, integration* or *polarity*, holds that a person is born with both masculine and feminine traits. A man supposedly could have been a man 250 times and a woman 250 times in previous incarnations, and the memory of those past life experiences are said to remain as indelible traces of consciousness. Thus, we are each a combination of male and female, masculine and feminine. The New Age encourages children and adults to appreciate and practice the harmony of opposites, teaching the individual to merge the two selves, man and woman.

Reincarnation and Incest

The regrettable reincarnation doctrine also encourages incest. Edgar Cayce, the famed "Sleeping Prophet" of the New Age, frequently gave psychic readings that would rationalize and explain away incestuous behavior. For example, if a father had sex with a young daughter, or a mother with a son, it might be explained away that the two human entities were husband and wife in a previous lifetime.

The implications of this teaching are both monstrous and monumental. Yet, Herbert Puryear, Ph.D., a devoted admirer of Edgar Cayce, while not advocating incest, nevertheless gives a nod of approval to Cayce's teachings on reincarnation that may well be used by others to justify this practice:

In a succession of incarnations in which the same entities are drawn together again and again, the respective relationships may be the same or they may vary. The Oedipus Rex story suggests a situation in which a man and woman are lovers in one incarnation. In a subsequent incarnation, the woman is the mother of the child who formerly was her lover.[38]

Cayce's teachings would even suggest that current family members—for example a brother and sister—may build up sexual desires which are then fulfilled in future incarnations (lifetimes). "The desire held," writes Puryear, "may bring the entities together again in a subsequent incarnation but they may come together under different family circumstances, such as sister and brother."[39]

Cayce's practice was to go into a deep trance-state during which his spirit guide would bring him a message. Cayce would then pass on the message as a "reading" to the person or persons he was counseling.

In one of Cayce's readings, he told a couple that in previous lifetimes they had "lived as father and daughter, as mother and son, as companions, as friends, as acquaintances." This confusion is actually, according to Cayce, grounds for a wonderful present marriage. "When a couple so blessed," he counseled, "recognize in themselves this opportunity, how gracious, how beautiful, how lovely is life itself. You have the opportunity, don't muff it!"[40]

Youth Incited to Revolt

Our young ones are not only being indoctrinated and introduced to immoral concepts of sexuality, they are also being enticed into open rebellion against parents. The New Age has for years kept up a constant, throbbing drumbeat to the ears of the young. Our teens are told that it is good to question authority and to revolt against parental and other forms of authority. Our young children are being slyly conditioned to believe that their parents' Christian beliefs are obsolete, old-fashioned, and even dangerous and inflammable. The evidence amply demonstrates that the aim of the New Age to alienate youth from their parents has been wildly successful and is now gaining further ground.

This strategy to incite our youth to revolt comes from many New Age sources. For instance, Foster Bailey, in *Running God's Plan*, declares: "Our youth are the victims of our degenerating civilization against which the best of them are rebelling."[41] "They are realizing," says Bailey, "that the God who never was is dead."[42]

Bailey is simply expressing the satanically inspired New Age view that as the old, outmoded Piscean age of Jesus degenerates and fades into oblivion, a shining and bright, Aquarian New Age is taking its place. The revolt of the youth, he explains, will help quicken the inevitable arrival of the gloriously brilliant "New Age of the Man-gods."

Another New Age authority promoting rebellion by youth against the older forces is Paula Tyler, an educator from Eureka Springs, Arkansas. Tyler has authored a revealing religious instruction guide for young people entitled, *New Age Metaphysics: An Introduction for Young Adults.* In it she cleverly gets across the point that young people should not hesitate to discard currently held beliefs inculcated by parents and others if they conflict with the New Age Worldview presented in the pages of her book:

> *If you don't like your life the way it is now, there are definite steps that can be taken to change it. . . . Often, without questioning, we have adopted the belief system of our parents. This review may disclose that these beliefs no longer work for us and need to be replaced by more positive ones. Once we have begun changing our beliefs, we can start to create our life the way we want it.*[43]

Will Youth Force the New Age Revolution on Their Parents?

Meanwhile, Omraam Aivankov, front man in the group known as the Universal White Brotherhood, writes in *Aquarius: Herald of the New Age* that it is the youth who will take up the mantle of leadership to *force* the older generation to accept the New Age Kingdom.[44] Aivankov insists that loyalty to Christianity, family, and country are a cancer. The revolutionary young, Aivankov says, will realize that Christianity is the road to war and that for world peace and harmony to succeed it is necessary to reject and discard Biblical Christianity:

> *We hold on to our old political and religious beliefs. Christians, for instance, are proud of belonging to the one true religion, of being the real sons of God whilst all the rest of us are heathens, miscreants, and heretics! It is too grotesque, too ridiculous. . . .*[45]

> *There is an entirely new effort being made today by young people; they will be the ones to force the adults to enlarge their concepts, because they will not put up with the old ways that create war. The young are on their way! They will turn the world upside down in Russia as well as in America; they will start a world revolution.*[46]

Aivankov and his fellow New Age workers in the "Universal White Brotherhood" intend to drive an irreconcilable wedge between youth and parents. Unmistakably, they are simply carrying out the odious hidden agenda of their masters in the spirit realm. As Aivankov himself admits, "The higher Intelligences and Beings are guiding humanity toward a goal we cannot even imagine."[47]

Perhaps Aivankov is telling the truth as he understands it. Perhaps he and many of his New Age cohorts *are*, ultimately, victims—unsuspecting, sincerely misguided disciples of demons who are leading them toward a goal they cannot even imagine. But the fact is, *if* those in the New Age had accepted Jesus Christ and His Word, they would not be so confused and uncertain about the goal of the New Age. They would know exactly *where* they are being guided—straight to hell and destruction.

The Truth is that the Bible exposes these "higher intelligences and beings" as Satan's agents, and it reveals their true objective—to bring mankind down with them into the pit.

PART V

How to Combat the New Age Flood of Filth

Spiritual warfare is the primary—and by far the most effective—method the Christian has in the fight to protect our families against New Age subversion and attack. And fervent prayer is the very essence of spiritual warfare. God wants us to go to Him in prayer with our requests and our needs. *Prayer changes things.*

Strangely, often when I advise a Christian to pray through a problem or to pray for help in difficult circumstances, I am met with a blank stare. "Isn't there *more* I can do?," I am asked, "Something more concrete, more practical?"

How odd that the Christian has access to the greatest Power in the galaxy, yet so often fails to go before the Master, Jesus Christ, and seek aid, comfort, and guidance!

So the most important thing we must keep in mind is that *prayer* changes things and is the chief weapon in our armory of Spiritual Warfare.

When we pray, what we really are doing is communicating directly with God who is Lord over all, *including* the devil. Some Christians mistakenly believe that in conducting Spiritual Warfare they must confront the devil head-on. They incorrectly conceive of Spiritual

Warfare as they themselves personally locking horns in a mighty, touch and go contest with demons and devils. But this is not the case. As Christians we are privileged to go before the throne of God Himself and seek *His* help. It is God who handles our fighting, who sees to our victory. And remember, He is not limited in ability. The cosmic struggle between good and evil, between God and the Adversary, is not an equal, tit-for-tat competition. *It's all one-sided, in God's favor.*

In essence, the question is, do you want to fruitlessly battle the devil and his New Age associates using your own, easily exhaustible strength, or . . . should you more wisely call on God and let Him do the infighting *for you?* The choice should be clear. Indeed, the Bible records that even the Archangel Michael, when directly confronted by the devil, did not attempt to fight using his own limited strength. Instead, exercising spiritual wisdom and judgment, he powerfully and with authority proclaimed, *"The Lord* rebuke you!"

> *Yet Michael the archangel, when contending with the devil he disputed about the body of Moses, durst not bring against him a railing accusation, but said, The Lord rebuke thee (Jude 9).*

The Christian parent's first responsibility is to put up a hedge of protection around his/her family. It is through prayer and by rebuking the devil's works, invoking the Lord's authority and might, that this hedge is erected. And it is by faith that the hedge remains in place.

Confrontation in the Ordinary World

While spiritual warfare is not to be neglected, the alert Christian should be aware that there are *also* concrete things that can be done to stem the tidal wave of New Age perversions. It is true that, gradually, our religious freedoms as American citizens are being steadily eroded. Yet, we still have at least *some* residue and vestiges of the constitutional liberty which we once so freely enjoyed. Therefore, let us, whenever possible, avail ourselves of these protections.

For example, in the 1970's, for awhile it seemed as though *transcendental meditation* (TM), as taught by the Hindu guru, Maharishi Mahesh Yogi, would literally become a staple in most American public schools. But then a small but brash courageous band of Christians decided to go to court and fight for their constitutional rights. They were determined to remove this disguised Hindu system of worship from their public school classrooms.

Finally, in the case of *Malnak v. Maharishi Mahesh Yogi,* October 19, 1977, the presiding judge ruled that TM was an inseparable part of the *Hindu* tradition and that because of its religious foundations, its presence in the public schools violated the establishment clause in the *First Amendment* to the *United States Constitution.*

Those who undergo TM training believe that they will gain the benefits of creativity, clear thinking, and—in the minds of many—self-divinity. However, there is absolutely no proof whatsoever of these claims. In fact, the scientific evidence available indicates that the regular practice of TM *diminishes* creative thinking and undermines sound, rational processes of the human mind. In reality, TM is simply a religious ritual in which the person prostrates himself or herself to a *Hindu guru*, chanting a mantra, or word, which in most cases is the name of a Hindu deity.

The Christians who stood up against this growing menace armed themselves with knowledge and the Truth. They used the system and they won. Christians may not, of course, be able to win every contest, but there is no logical reason and certainly no spiritual justification for the Christian to apathetically lay around and shrink from the battle. The stakes are too high for that. Moreover, God's Word tells us that faith without works is dead! (see James 2:26)

Tackling New Age Discrimination Against Christians

Another great victory for Christians—and thus for America and the family—came in 1988 in a ruling by the Equal Employment Opportunity Commission (EEOC) in Washington, D.C. Because so many Christians had complained to the EEOC that they were being forced by their employers to attend New Age-oriented training courses and seminars, the EEOC, after careful deliberation and investigation, issued ruling number N-915.022, dated February, 1988.

This broad and inclusive ruling is sweeping in its consequences. It prohibits employers from *requiring* Christians or other workers to attend any training that would infringe on their religious convictions—*even if the training is not labeled New Age.*

In other words, now Christians have the authoritative backing and protection of the most powerful agency in government devoted to protecting workers from discrimination in the work place.

Unfortunately, the mass media—TV networks, newspaper and magazines—because they are owned and influenced by the New Age leadership—have conveniently refused to publicize this important ruling by the EEOC. Few people even know that such a ruling exists. Therefore, I have included in the back pages of this book (see Appendix 1) the entire text of the *EEOC Notice* that officially announced that agency's findings and ruling regarding New Age training programs. My prayer and hope is that Christians everywhere will use this document as ammunition, enabling them to stand up for their rights by rejecting unconstitutional mind control training.

New Age Methods and Ideas in our Schools

Keep in mind, too, that if New Age techniques, ideas, and instruction cannot legally be imposed on *adults* on their jobs, it stands to reason that these same New Age practices should not be required anywhere else either.

Public schools come immediately to mind: if *adults* cannot be forced to submit to New Age instruction, what possible justification do teachers and school administrators have for subjecting our *children* to such instruction?

To Aid You in Your Efforts ...

To successfully aid you as a Christian in your fight against New Age encroachment on our freedoms, I have also included two other appendices. Appendix 2 is a three page chart, originally published in my book, *New Age Cults and Religions*, which contrasts the false teachings of the New Age with Biblical truths. Appendix 3 is a list of terms frequently used in the New Age movement. This should give you a clue as to when New Age ideas are being expressed. However, mere use of any of these terms does not necessarily imply New Age influence, so the context of their use must also be considered.

Government Study Concludes: New Age Methods Totally Worthless!

Did you know that a massive, government-funded study has found that almost all the New Age techniques and methods now in use in many of our public schools and in our workplaces *are of absolutely no value whatsoever?* Included in the ineffective and worthless category are such highly touted techniques as *visualization, meditation, biofeedback, yoga, neurolinguistic programming (self-talk), split brain (left brain/right brain) learning, accelerated learning methods, stress reduction and relaxation techniques, ESP, parapsychology, levitation, out-of-body experiences, psychic healing, etc.*

Now there is iron-clad documentation for those who want to confront school boards, employers, government agencies, and so forth with undeniable, irrefutable, absolute proof that they're not only wasting our hard-earned tax dollars on such rubbish, but also wreaking havoc and damage on people's minds. Our children's minds are especially at risk.

This important study I am referring to is the National Research Council's 1988 report on *Enhancing Human Performance.*

This comprehensive report is based on *three full years of active study* by the National Academy of Sciences, as well as a thorough review of all other scientific studies conducted on these subjects for the past 130 years! It was funded by the U.S. Army which asked the National Academy of Sciences "to examine the potential value of certain techniques that had been proposed to enhance human performance." (Many New Age groups had for a number of years encouraged the U.S. Army to adopt such techniques.)

In 1985 The National Academy of Sciences appointed a prestigious 14-member committee, the members of which represented such disciplines as physiology; clinical, social, and industrial psychology; cognitive neuroscience, and education. These learned scientists were of the highest caliber and their voluminous study took three years and $500,000 to complete.

What were the revealing findings of this distinguished scientific panel? Simply this: that there is not one iota of evidence to support any of all the numerous New Age "techniques." Not one shred of proof. *Not one!* For example, the report concluded:

The committee finds no scientific justification from research conducted over a period of 130 years . . .

> *While often using the language of science to justify their approach, these (New Age and human potential) promoters are for the most part not trained professionals in the social and behavioral sciences.*

New Age Leaders in a State of Shock

Leaders of New Age and "human potential" organizations are in a state of shock over this official government report. They definitely *do not want* the results of this study to get out to the general public. They know that if this happens they'll lose their lucrative money contracts. You see, they are now being paid big bucks for all the worthless instruction they are now "providing" our unwitting school districts, corporations, and other buyers of these useless mental gymnastic exercises. New Age and human potential promoters are especially alarmed over the statement by the committee appointed by the National Academy of Sciences that, *"Virtually all further research in the selected areas of its inquiry would be worthless."*

The New Age and human potential propagandists well know that their long ride on the money gravy train will end as soon as the public discovers the shocking truth. That truth is contained in the National Academy of Science's findings that the techniques and methods studied were so devoid of value that, although "the claimed phenomena and applications range from the incredible to the outrageously incredible," nevertheless "nothing approaching a scientific literature supports the claims."

In reporting the committee's findings that the New Age techniques are worthless, the distinguished chairman of the National Research Council (NRC), John Swets, stated: "The underlying theme that emerges from our study is that there are no easy ways or fixes for helping people perform more effectively."

Given the results of this first-ever exhaustive study, I highly encourage Christians to boldly resist all efforts by public schools, corporations and employers, government agencies, universities, colleges, and other groups to saddle us with mindless, unproductive, money-wasting New Age instruction of all kinds. Keep in mind, too, that much of this defective instruction does not come labeled as "New Age."

The results of the study by the National Academy of Sciences was briefly mentioned in *Science News*, Jan. 2, 1988, p. 9. The full, book-length report, entitled *Enhancing Human Performance*, can be ordered from the National Academy Press, 2101 Constitution Ave., N.W., Washington, D.C. 20418 [phone (202) 334-3313]. Each copy is $22.50 (paperback).

The Sovereignty of God

The New Age has come so far so fast that unless we put things in perspective it is easy for us to assume that all is lost. *All* is *not lost*. The Word of God assures us that Satan's victory will be short-lived. The Plan will ultimately fail.

Because we are Christians, Jesus has given us freedom from worry. We know that He who is within us is greater than he who is in the world. God is our victorious, all-conquering King. Paul spoke to this in these uplifting words:

> *Who shall separate us from the love of Christ? . . .*
> *I am persuaded, that neither death, nor life, nor*
> *angels, nor principalities, nor powers, nor things*
> *present, nor things to come, nor height, nor depth,*
> *nor any other creature, shall be able to separate us*
> *from the love of God, which is in Christ Jesus our*
> *Lord. (Romans 8:35-39)*

So we are not fearful for ourselves. Our joyous fate is sealed by the grace of the Lord. But we can rightly be anxious over what might befall our loved ones, neighbors, and friends—and all of mankind—who, because they do not know Jesus, do not possess eternal security.

The emergence on the world scene of what could well be the prophesied, end-time Satanic religious system can in one sense be viewed as positive, for it signals the imminent return of Jesus Christ and heralds the Kingdom of God that is soon to come. But our hearts grow heavy when as Christians we realize the harvest is drawing near and there is so little time to warn the lost and bring to them the blessed message of salvation. The New Age World Religion should provide incentive for Christians to boldly preach the gospel and to earnestly spread the good news that the time of man's deliverance is truly at hand.

A Sure Formula For Success

I have prayerfully asked God to reveal to me what I should say to concerned Christians who ask, "What can I do about The Plan of the New Age to destroy Christianity and put man under bondage?" The Lord has answered my prayers, and I would now like to share with you the four positive steps that you and every Christian can take in this time of crisis and turmoil.

Step 1: *Read and study your Holy Bible so you will be knowledgeable of God's Word and invulnerable to New Age distortions and unholy claims.*

While all around us, muddled intellectuals and mixed-up men and women are, figuratively speaking, "losing their heads," we should keep ours clear by strengthening our minds with the wisdom of the Book of Books. The warfare for man's soul involves a series of battles over *doctrine*, and if Christians are to save as many of the lost as possible, we must be girded with God's truth. Our footing must be sure as we engage the enemies of the Scripture.

Step 2: *Put Jesus first in your life and make soul-winning for Christ your top priority.*

When we put Jesus first in our own lives and make soul-winning our top priority, all the forces of hell cannot withstand us. Christians who affirm and commit themselves and their churches to what has been called the "irreducible minimums" will serve as shining beacons of light to lost souls. These include the primacy of the Bible as the inspired, inerrant Word of God, an unshakable belief in the divinity of Jesus Christ, and the acceptance of Jesus Christ as the only way to salvation.

Step 3: *Confront and fight New Age apostasy wherever you find it, understanding that Jesus is Lord and that He will prevail. Use prayer as both a resource and a powerful vehicle to ward off God's enemies.*

In the Epistle of Jude we find the admonition that we should "earnestly contend for the faith which was once delivered unto the saints." Jude told us to look for "certain men crept in unawares, who were before of old ordained to this condemnation, ungodly men, turning the grace of our God into lasciviousness, and denying the only Lord God, and our Lord Jesus Christ" (Jude 1:3, 4).

What a powerful message for today! Earnestly contend for the faith! Listen also to what James told us: "resist the devil, and he will flee from you" (James 4:7). How do we go about this?

The Bible provides the answer. James told us to be soul-winners, to convert the lost: "Let him know, that he which converteth the sinner from the error of his way shall save a soul from death, and shall hide a multitude of sins" (James 5:20).

Be assured that in witnessing for Christ, you will be going up against the strongholds of Satan. You will also, on many occasions, be locked in battle with the evil "wisdom" of those promoting New Age doctrines and falsehoods. The Bible tells us that we must not wish men of evil Godspeed (2 John 10, 11). Theirs is a mean-spirited goal, and we must not be tolerant toward a belief system which has as its principal aim the poisoning of souls. Our right attitude should be one of "tough love": we love the individual, but we deeply regret and reject his awful message.

Confrontation with evil cannot be won without prayer. The Christian who prays constantly and meditates on God's Word will find that his actions and words are imbued with great power from the Holy Spirit. Always remember that Jesus has already proven victorious. We're not on the winning side. *We're on the side that won!*

Step 4: *Reach out in Christian love to individuals in the New Age Movement, many of whom are confused, hungry for spiritual things, and searching for truth. Show them that Jesus Christ is the answer and that He loves them.*

Though Satan is the very foundation-stone for the New Age World Religion, we must be very careful about our attitude toward New Age believers. By no means is every person involved in the New Age Movement calculatingly evil. Most people entangled in this movement are themselves victims. Some are earnestly searching for the truth and are spiritually hungry. Also, many are motivated by sincere humanitarianism; but being mentally confused, these individuals are deluded by New Age gurus and teachers. A great number may not even be fully aware of The Plan which Satan and New Age human leaders have conceived for man's future. While we abhor the un-Christian tenets of New Age believers, we must always keep uppermost in our minds the fact that Jesus died for *their* sins as well as our own.

This is why I encourage Christians to reach out to New Agers in love and to counteract this apostasy with all the spiritual weapons that Jesus so richly provides us, including prayer, reading God's Holy Word, Christian example, and— most important of all—faith.

99

PART VI

How to Defeat the New Age: Guidelines for Overcomers

The evidence is undeniable that Christian families, and especially our kids, have been targeted by the leaders of the New Age. We, after all, are the *only opposition* to the triumph of evil in this world. We are the ones who worship, represent, and bring His light to the lost and to those deceived by the adversary. Thus, we are his most feared enemy. Yet, even though we are the devil's chief enemy, there is victory for us in that God has made us overcomers. We are the unconquerable, the eternal, the ones who cannot be defeated.

If we but place our trust in God, our families will be protected from the New Age scourge. Yes, the devil may at times gain temporary advantage. But we must stand fast, pray, have faith . . . and, on occasion, practice patience and endurance. Victory is assured for God's own.

Keep in mind, nevertheless, that in overcoming the New Age, in protecting our families, we will suffer attacks and sometimes even vicious opposition. But if we persevere, we will be victorious.

Six Obstacles In Your Way

Now, there are six things that you and I should expect when we determine to oppose the evils of this age. I list these six obstacles below because I want you to be ever vigilant and ever ready when the foe mounts an offensive against you. That being said, here are the six things to expect as you do God's will:

1. *The world will oppose you.* Don't think it strange, the Apostle Peter advised the Church, when fiery trials come your way. The world mocked and ridiculed Jesus. They'll mock and ridicule *you.* The world especially enjoys ridiculing those who believe in Bible prophecy and hold on to the promise of Jesus' second coming. Expect to receive scorn, laughter, scoffing, sneers. Count them a blessing, for Jesus taught that "Blessed are you when men persecute you for righteousness' sake."

2. *Lukewarm Christians will oppose you.* Uncommitted Christians who have joined hands with the world will join in the campaign to ridicule you and discredit your testimony. Their complacency and opposition perhaps hurt the most, but, still, don't give up the fight! Pray for them, that their eyes will be opened.

3. *Greedy people will oppose you.* Crooks, frauds, cheats, and deceivers abound in the New Age. Many pawn off New Age ideas and techniques as "holistic," healthy, and psychologically sound. Through their seminars and counseling they profit from the New Age. Expect their determined opposition when you unmask their work.

4. *Compromisers will oppose you.* Just like the lukewarm Christians, these people will accuse you of "injuring the cause of *unity.*" They will brand you as intolerant, narrow-minded, and bigoted. Jesus was likewise labeled, so . . . what's new?

5. *People will talk about you.* When you defend yourself and your family against New Age encroachment, enemies will misrepresent what you say. They'll exaggerate, lie and bear false witness. You'll most probably be called a trouble-maker, and you'll be identified as a person who's against what's best for society. You may even be characterized as a child abuser (because you insist on teaching your children Biblical principles) or as a "homophobe" (because you remind others of what the Bible says about homosexuality and lesbianism).

6. *False doctrine will raise its ugly head as so-called Christian pastors and teachers oppose your efforts.* They'll suggest you are unloving, unkind, unspiritual, ignorant, uncouth, uneducated and (yikes!) . . . a "fundamentalist."

False teachers can build huge congregations and draw financial support by compromising on the Word of God. Jesus was bitterly opposed by the established Church of His day. You, too, will discover that the established "Church" will prefer to support the New Age because today's compromising leaders find it profitable to do so. Meanwhile, they'll give comfort and aid to the adversary by either excommunicating you or publicly degrading and criticizing your courageous stance for the Truth.

God's Strength is Our Armor

Again, this opposition comes with the territory for a Christian. Expect it, anticipate it, prepare for it. It will come. But it should not deter you. Why? Because God's strength will be your armor, His Word your companion.

God has appointed you and I as watchmen on the wall, set to defend the faith. Let us, therefore, stay constant. Let us watch and pray. And let us never forget that the struggle is worth it. God is faithful. He knows how to reward His own!

APPENDIX 1

EEOC Ruling on New Age Training Programs

ee⊛c U.S. Equal Employment
Opportunity Commission

FOR IMMEDIATE RELEASE
Friday, April 1, 1988

CONTACT: Deborah J. Graham
Margaret Fernandez
(202) 634-6036
(202) 634-7057 (TDD)

EEOC SAYS 'NEW AGE' TRAINING PROGRAMS MAY CONFLICT WITH EMPLOYEES' RELIGIOUS BELIEFS
* * * * *
Issues Guidance to Field Offices on Handling Cases

WASHINGTON -- The U.S. Equal Employment Opportunity Commission
on Feb. 22 issued a policy statement on employer-conducted "new age"
training programs to provide guidance to EEOC investigators in
handling cases where an employee objects to the program or aspects
of the program on grounds that they conflict with the employee's
religious beliefs.

"New age" training programs are designed to improve employee
motivation, cooperation or productivity through techniques such as
meditation, yoga and biofeedback.

The issue of "new age" programs, EEOC says, can be resolved
under the traditional Title VII theory of religious accommodation
which states that an employer must provide reasonable accommodation
for an employee's or prospective employee's religious needs unless
to do so would create undue hardship on the conduct of the
employer's business. If an employee notifies an employer that his or
her religious beliefs conflict with some aspect of a "new age"
training program, an employer may accommodate the employee's beliefs
by substituting an alternative technique or method not offensive to
the employee's beliefs or by excusing the employee from that
particular part of the training program.

Whether or not the employer believes there is a religious basis
for or content to the training or techniques used is irrelevant to
determining the need for accommodation, EEOC states. The employer
may only consider the sincerity with which the employee holds the
expressed beliefs.

- over -

An employee has complained, for example, that a training exercise involving·self-hypnosis conflicted with his religion which teaches that a person should always be in control of his or her thoughts in order to make correct moral choices.

EEOC enforces Title VII of the Civil Rights Act of 1964 prohibiting employment discrimination based on race, color, religion, sex or national origin, the Age Discrimination in Employment Act, the Equal Pay Act and prohibitions against federal sector discrimination affecting individuals with handicaps.

###

MAR. 22

	NOTICE	NUMBER N-915.022
		DATE 2/88

1. SUBJECT: Policy statement on "new age" training programs which conflict with employees' religious beliefs.

2. PURPOSE: This policy statement is intended to provide guidance in the handling of cases where an employee objects to participating in a training program because it utilizes techniques or exercises which conflict with the employee's religious beliefs.

3. EFFECTIVE DATE: Upon receipt.

4. EXPIRATION DATE:

5. ORIGINATOR: TITLE VII/EPA Division, Office of Legal Counsel.

6. INSTRUCTIONS: This notice supplements the instructions in § 628 of Volume II of the Compliance Manual, Religious Accommodation, and should be inserted after p. 628-20.

I. Introduction

Employers are increasingly making use of training programs designed to improve employee motivation, cooperation, or productivity through the use of various so-called "new age" techniques. 1/ For example, a large utility company requires its employees to attend seminars based on the teachings of a mystic, George Gurdjieff, which the company claims has helped improve communications among employees. 2/ Another corporation provides its employees with workshops in stress management using so called "faith healers" who read the "auras" of employees and contact the body's "fields of energy" to improve the health of its employees. 3/ Specialists in employee training say that "most of the nation's major corporations and numerous government agencies have hired some consultants and purveyors of similar 'personal growth' training programs in recent years." 4/ The programs utilize a wide variety of techniques: meditation, guided visualization, self-hypnosis, therapeutic touch, biofeedback, yoga, walking on fire, and inducing altered states of consciousness. 5/ These programs focus on changing individual employees' attitudes and self-concepts by promoting increased self-esteem, assertiveness, independence, and creativity

---

1/ Gurus Hired to Motivate Workers Are Raising Fears of 'Mind Control,' (hereinafter Gurus) New York Times, April 17, 1987, at A-18; New Age Harmonies, Time Mag., Dec. 7, 1987 at 62.

2/ Gurus, supra, n. 1.

3/ New Age Harmonies, supra, n. 1 at 62-63.

4/ Gurus, supra, n. 1.

5/ New Age Harmonies, supra, n. 1 at 64, 69.

DISTRIBUTION: CM HOLDERS   EEOC FORM 156, MAR 87

in order to improve overall productivity. 6/ Some employees have objected to participating in these programs because they view them as promoting values different from their own and as conflicting with their religious beliefs. 7/ One employee objected that a training program he was ordered to attend using meditation and guided visualization could change a person's view of reality and religious beliefs. 8/ Another employee argued that a training program that "focused everything on the self" as the center and source of energy conflicted with his belief that human fate is dependent on the "will of God." 9/

Although the courts and the Commission have not addressed the particular conflicts raised by the "new age" training programs, this issue can be re-solved under the traditional Title VII theory of religious accommodation. The disagreement over whether the training programs are religious raises the question of whether an employee must prove that some aspect of the training program is actually based on religion or has religious content in order to establish a need for religious accommodation. It is necessary, therefore, to examine the nature of an employee's religious belief requiring accommodation under Title VII, as well as the nature of an employer's duty to accommodate a religious belief.

II.   The Nature of Religious Belief Under Title VII

The Commission defines religious practices to include moral or ethical beliefs as to what is right or wrong which are sincerely held with the strength of traditional religious views. 10/ This is adopted from the Supreme Court's determination in Seeger that religion need only be "[a] sincere and meaningful belief which occupies in the life of its possessor a place parallel to that filled by ... God [in other religions]." 11/ Even those religious beliefs that others may find "incomprehensible or incorrect" are protected under Title VII. 12/ Therefore, an employer may not judge the veracity or reasonableness

6/ Gurus, supra, n. 1.

7/ Id.

8/ Id.

9/ Id.

10/ Guidelines on Discrimination Because of Religion, 29 C.F.R. § 1605.1, "Reli-gious" nature of a practice or belief.

11/ Commission Decision No. 76-104, CCH EEOC Decisions (1983) ¶ 6500 (The Commis-sion determined that if religion were construed more narrowly for Title VII pur-poses than it is in the context of § 6(j) of the Military Training and Service Act, then Title VII's proscription of religious discrimination would conflict with the First Amendment's Establishment Clause), citing United States v. Seeger, 380 U.S. 163, 176 (1965) (the Court defines religion under § 6(j) of the Universal Military Training and Service Act, 50 U.S.C.A. App. § 456(j) (1968); see Compliance Manual § 628.4(b), "Religious" Nature of a Practice or Belief, p. 628-4.

12/ See Commission Decision No. 76-104, CCH EEOC Decisions (1983) ¶ 6500, citing Welsh v. United States, 90 S. Ct. 1792, 1796 (1970).

2

of the religious beliefs of an employee. 13/ A religious belief or practice need not be based upon a traditional religion 14/ and does not have to be a belief held as a tenet by others of the same religion. 15/ Moreover, the Commission has held that protected religious belief also includes the freedom not to believe. 16/ The only limitations on a belief protected under Title VII are that it must be religious as opposed to social, political, or economic in nature 17/ and it must be sincerely held. 18/

That the employer or the sponsor of a "new age" program believes there is no religious basis for, or content to, the training or techniques used is irrelevant to determining the need for accommodation. If an employee believes that some aspect of the training program conflicts with his/her own beliefs, an employer may only inquire as to what the employee's beliefs are and consider the sincerity with which the employee holds those beliefs. The employer may not base its decision to accommodate the employee's religious beliefs on its (the employer's) own evaluation of whether the training or the techniques used actually conflict with the employee's religious beliefs. An employer may not reject an employee's request for accommodation on the basis that the employee's beliefs about the "new age" training seem unreasonable.

13/ See Callan v. Woods, 663 F.2d 679, 685 (9th Cir. 1981) (held "in applying the free exercise clause of the First Amendment, courts may not inquire into the truth, validity, or reasonableness of a claimant's religious beliefs,"); United States v. Rasheed, 663 F.2d 843, 847 (9th Cir. 1981) (validity of religious beliefs cannot be questioned); (note that since the Commission has adopted the standards enunciated by the Supreme Court in Seeger and Welsh, guidance can also be obtained from lower courts applying the same rule).

14/ Commission Decision No. 81-33, CCH EEOC Decisions (1983) ¶ 6828 (CP who sincerely holds a belief with the strength of traditional religious views does not have to prove that others hold or share his belief); 29 CFR § 1605.1.

15/ Thomas v. Review Board of Indiana Employment Security Division, 450 U.S. 707, 715-16, 25 EPD ¶ 31,622 (1981) (religious beliefs need not be universally held within religion in order to qualify as religious or in order to be entitled to protection); 29 CFR ¶ 1605.1.

16/ Commission Decision No. 72-1114, CCH EEOC Decisions (1973) ¶ 6347 (however, the Title VII protection which is given to those who have chosen not to believe is only applicable to those who choose not to believe in a particular religious practice, belief, or in religion itself); see Young v. Southwestern Savings and Loan Association, 509 F.2d 140, 9 EPD ¶ 9995 (5th Cir. 1975) (supervisor told employee that she had a duty to attend staff meetings at which prayer and devotionals were conducted; held, employer obligated to accommodate employee's religious beliefs which include the freedom not to believe).

17/ See Seeger, 380 U.S. at 173; see also United States v. MacIntosh, 283 U.S. 605, 633-634 (1931); for an example, see Compliance Manual § 628.4(2), p. 628-6.

18/ United States v. Rasheed, 663 F.2d 843, 847 (9th Cir. 1981) (although the validity of religious beliefs cannot be questioned, the sincerity of the person claiming to hold such beliefs can be examined," citing Seeger, 380 U.S. at 185); see Compliance Manual § 628(b)(2), p. 628-5, for instructions for determining whether a religious practice or belief requires protection.

3

EEOC RULING ON NEW AGE TRAINING PROGRAMS

III. Employer's duty to accommodate

Under § 701(j) of Title VII an employer must provide reasonable accommodation for an employee's or prospective employee's religious needs unless to do so would create an undue hardship on the conduct of the employer's business. [19] The need for accommodation most frequently arises where an individual's religious belief, observances, or practices conflict with a specific task or requirement of the employee's job. For example, an employee may object to participating in a training exercise involving self-hypnosis because his religion teaches that a person should always be in control of his/her thoughts in order to make correct moral choices. The employer's duty to accommodate will usually entail making a special exception from or adjustment to the particular training requirement so that the employee is able to comply with the dictates of his/her religious beliefs.

Where an employee notifies an employer that his/her religious beliefs conflict with a particular training technique or method used in a "new age" training program, an employer may accommodate the employee's belief by substituting an alternative technique or method not offensive to the employee's belief or by excusing the employee from that particular part of the training program. The employer may have to excuse the employee from the entire program where the employee contends that the program itself is based on a concept contrary to his/her beliefs, unless the employer can show undue hardship. [20] Because an employer may not impose any religious requirements on the terms or conditions of employment, an employer who in any way penalizes an employee who has been excused from participating in a training program because of religious conflicts discriminates on the basis of religion. Moreover, an employer may be required to provide alternative training as part of reasonably accommodating the employee's religious beliefs unless it can show undue hardship. Exempting an employee from a training program without providing alternative training may disadvantage the employee with respect to his/her employment opportunities.

> Example : R requires its employees, as part of a training program, to participate in a form of meditation that involves emptying one's mind of all thoughts by repeating a meaningless word. CP objects to participating in this

---

[19] 42 U.S.C. §2000(e)(j) (1976); 29 CFR § 1605.2(b)(1).

[20] The mere assumption that many more people with the same religious belief as the individual may also need accommodation is not sufficient evidence of undue hardship. See Commission Decisions Nos. 81-83 and 72-0606, at CCH EEOC Decisions ¶ 6828 (1983) and ¶ 6310 (1973) and Compliance Manual § 628.7(a), pp. 628-23 & 24.

4

AMERICA SHATTERED

exercise because it conflicts with his religious belief that a person should always keep his mind open to "divine inspiration." R must accommodate CP's religious belief by excusing him from this exercise even though R, the sponsor of the training program, and other employees believe that this form of meditation does not conflict with any religious beliefs.

The employer may also be liable where the training program is explicitly based upon religious beliefs. 21/ Under Title VII an employer is obligated to maintain a working environment free of coercion or intimidation based on religion. 22/ In this situation, an employer discriminates not only against employees and potential employees whose individual religious beliefs conflict with the training program but also against employees and potential employees who choose not to have religious beliefs.

> Example : R requires its employees, as part of a training program, to participate in a form of meditation that involves emptying one's mind of all thoughts by repeating a meaningless word. The employees are taught that this meditation will bring them into contact with the "ultimate reality of the universe" which empowers them to reach the "supreme authentication" of their "True Self" and to become one with "All That That Is." R must accommodate the

---

21/ See C.D. No. 72-0528, CCH EEOC Decisions (1973) ¶ 6316 (R has continuing policy of conducting, on its premises and during regular work hours, a weekly meeting which includes prayer recitals, hymn singing and sermons from local clergymen; all employees, regardless of individual religious persuasion or moral code, are urged to attend; R's policy on its face discriminates against all employees and potential employees who do not desire to attend such meetings because of their individual religious beliefs or lack of any religious beliefs); State of Minnesota v. Sports & Health Club, 392 N.W.2d 320, 41 EPD ¶ 36,617 (1986) (employer permitted only born again Christians to hold management positions, required managers to attend weekly Bible studies, and suggested that other personnel also attend; held employer wrongfully imposed religious beliefs on employees); Young v. Southwestern Savings and Loan Association, supra note 16.

22/ Commission Decision No. 72-1114, CCH EEOC Decisions (1973) ¶ 6347 (R's failure to provide a working environment free of religious intimidation is violative of Section 703(a) of Title VII: CP's supervisor discussed his religious convictions with CP and other employees on the job).

5

religious beliefs of its employees by excusing from this exercise, not only those employees who object because this conflicts with their religious beliefs, but also employees who object because they have chosen not to have religious beliefs. In addition, R's policy of requiring employees to attend a religiously oriented program discriminates on its face against all employees and potential employees on the basis of religion.

The issue of "new age" training programs is Non-CDP. Charges involving this issue should be sent to Headquarters until further notice. Contact Coordination and Guidance Services at FTS 634-6423 for instructions.

2/22/88
Date

Approved _Clarence Thomas_
Clarence Thomas
Chairman

6

113

APPENDIX 2

The New Age vs. True Christianity: A Contrast

New Age vs. True Christianity
A Contrast

New Age Teaching	Bible Teaching
1. "God" is the creation and creator, the All-in-One. He/She/It is the Divine Intelligence and the Creative Force.	1. God is separate from, greater than, and Master of His creation (Acts 17:28; Col. 1:16-17; I Cor. 4:7; Gen. 1:1; Isa. 48:11-12).
2. God and the Holy Spirit are impersonal: a presence, a vibration, an energy force, universal law, Universal Mind, Cosmic Consciousness, Divine Presence, Eternal Reality, Real Presence, Creative Force, Cosmic One, etc.	2. God is "Personal." Though a spirit, He is infinite, is eternally transcendent (external to man) and worthy of our worship. (John 1; 16:13-14; Rev. 4:11).
3. Each human being is endowed with a spark of divinity. An illumined, or enlightened, person is beyond such moral distinctions as "good" or "bad."	3. Humanity is fallen, born in bondage to sin, and in need of redemption. Satan is real and evil exists. Man can become free of the condemnation of sin through Jesus Christ. (Rom. 3:23; John 3:16-19, 8:44; Jer. 17:5-9; Eph. 2:8-9; Rev. 20).
4. Jesus did not die for the sins of the world. His shedding of blood, though tragic, is irrelevant to man's spiritual needs today. No atonement. Christianity is a "bloody religion."	4. Jesus died on the cross as a sin sacrifice. Through His blood we are saved and through His resurrection we are assured of eternal life and victory over death. (Heb. 9:22; Matt. 26-28; John 3:16; Rom. 3:23; Gal. 1:1-5; 2 Cor. 5:21; Eph 2:8-9).

New Age Teaching (continued)	Bible Teaching (continued)
5. Jesus was *a* god, *a* Christ, *a* perfect Master, *a* man who earned his divinity, a perfected man, *a* messenger of God, *a* prophet of God; He was as much God as are all of us.	5. Jesus is, was, and forever shall be God Almighty, the one true God; and there is no other besides Him. Jesus created all things. He, the Father, and the Holy Spirit are eternally One. They cannot be separated--ever. There is but *one* Godhead. Jesus is the only Christ. (1 John 2:20-25; Heb. 1:8; Col. 1:14-19, 2:9-10).
6. Man must take responsibility for his problems and forgive himself. There is no one outside of man to whom we must plead for forgiveness, no one outside of ourselves who *can* forgive us.	6. A loving God can forgive our sins and cleanse us. He offers man the free gift of salvation. (1 Peter 1; 1 John 1:2-6, 3:16; James 4:6-11).
7. Man must endure many life cycles (reincarnation) until his karma is cleansed, pure spirit is achieved, and union with "God" is attained.	7. Man has only one physical life on earth. Upon death, man returns to God, the Creator, who is our Judge. Those saved escape condemnation and receive eternal life. (John 3:16; Heb. 9:27).
8. Through good works and/or enlightenment, man can aspire to divinity and union with "God" (all that is). This is the universal law.	8. Man is not saved by Law or through his good works. Nor can man become enlightened through his own efforts. Eternal life and heaven are free gifts given by a loving, personal God to those who accept His grace and are thus born again. (Gal. 3:1-4, 2:16; Titus 3:5; John 3:3).
9. Eating meat produces negative karma in a person. Meat is forbidden and the (enlightened) superior spiritual being does not eat meat (vegetarianism).	9. God blesses all things He has created for man to eat, including meat. (Col. 2:16; I Tim. 4:3).

New Age Teaching *(continued)*

10. Spirit beings, or entities, are able to provide spiritual insight and guidance. They are helpers who can show man how to become fully conscious and realize self (become divine).

11. The Holy Bible is insufficient as a guide for man. Other "bibles" from other religions, ancient religious texts and writings, and fresh new revelations either from people living today or spirit entities are equally as valuable and reliable.

12. Man is part of and one with the creation; the creation is "God;" thus man is also "God." He is co-creator of the universe. Through an evolutionary process, man is "awakening" and returning to godhood.

Bible Teaching *(continued)*

10. There is only one mediator between man and God—Christ Jesus. Communication with spirit guides and entities is an occult practice called necromancy. It is an abomination to God. Such spirits are unclean and not of God. (Deut. 18:10-12; I Tim. 4:1; Isa. 8:19; I Sam. 28:1-25; I Chr. 10:13-14).

11. The Bible is authoritative, powerful, and able to guide man in every aspect of his life, producing joy and satisfaction in the reader who knows Christ as Lord. (Rev. 22:18-19; John 5:39; Acts 17:2, 11; 18:28; Rom. 15:4; 16:26; II Pet. 1:21).

12. God is the great I AM—transcendent to His creation, magnificent, glorious, King of kings. Man is made to serve God. Someday, every knee will bow and every tongue confess that Jesus Christ is Lord. (Phillip. 5:2-13; Rev. 22:18-19; John 5:39; Rev. 21:1-8, 22:8-9; Matt. 18:3; John 3:3, 14:6).

Reprinted from *New Age Cults and Religions*, by Texe Marrs
© 1990 Living Truth Publishers, 8103 Shiloh Court, Austin, Texas 78745

APPENDIX 3

New Age Terminology

Abortion
Acupressure
Acupuncture
Adept
Age of Aquarius
Ageless Wisdom
Agni Point
Ajna Centre
Alcoholism as "Sacred Disease"
Alice Bailey Writings
Altered States of Consciousness
American Indian Medicine
Amulets/Talismans
Ancient Wisdom, The
Animism
Ankh Symbol
Anthroposophy
Antichrist and 666
Antisemitism
Aquarian Gospel
Aquarian Age
Arcane
Artemis
Aryan
Ascended Masters
Ashram
Astral Body
Astral Travel
Astral Projection
Astrology/Zodiac
Atlantis/Lemuria Continents
Atman

Aura Readings
Aura
Avatar
Awaken Kundalini
Awaken to Divinity
Baal
Bates Method, The
Bioenergy
Bi-Sexuality
Body Energy Fields
Breathe-in God
Buddhism
Bull Dancing
Camelot
Centering
Centers of Light
Chakras
Channeling of Spirits
Chanting
Charms
Chelas
Christ Consciousness
Christian Rock Music/Christian
    Science
Church Universal and
    Triumphant
Collective Consciousness
Color Therapy
Cosmic Fire
Cosmic Energy
Cosmic Consciousness
Counterculture

Course in Miracles, A (the book)
Creative Intelligence, The
Creative Visualization
Crone
Crystals
Dance of Life, The
Death Education
Deathing
Decreeing
Demonic Tongues
Demons
Dervish Dances
Devas
Diamond in the Lotus
Dianetics
Divine Wisdom
Divinity of Man
Dominion Theology
Dragon
Druids
Dungeons and Dragons
Earth is Divine
Earth Religion
Earth Worship
Eastern Mysticism
Eckankar
Edgar Cayce
Egyptian Art
Embrace the Darkness
Empty One's Mind
Enchantment
Energy Point
Esoteric
EST
Ether World
Euthanasia
Evolution
Expanded Awareness
Familiar Spirits
Fire Walking

Force, The
Fortune Telling
Forum, The
Gaia (Earth Goddess)
Gestalt Psychology
Global Healing
Global Mind-Link
Globalism
Gnosis
God Consciousness
God of Forces
Goddess Worship
Godlike Powers
Great Invocation, The
Guided Imagery
Guru
Harmonic Convergence
Heal Mother Earth
Healing of Memories
Hermaphrodite
Hierarchy, The
High Religion
Higher Consciousness
Higher Self
Hinduism
Holistic Health
Holistic Medicine
Holy Grail
Homeopathy
Homosexuality/Lesbianism
Horus
Hypnosis
I Ching
I Am Movement
Incense
Indian Rituals
Initiation Inner Healer
Inner Knowledge
Inner Light
Inner Healing

Inner Space
Inner Child
Inner Guide
Inner Teacher
Inner Plane
Interconnectedness
Invisible Guides
Iridology
Isis
Jesus a Way-Shower
Jewish Kabbala
Journey of Life, The
Jungian Psychology/Carl Jung
Jungian Archetypes
Karma (Law of)
Karmic
Keys of Enoch
King Arthur and Court
Kingdom Now!
Krishna
Kroning
Kundalini
Law of One, The
Lemuria
Levitation
Ley Lines
Lord Maitreya
Lotus
LSD and other Mind Drugs
Lucifer Worship (Lightbearer)
Luciferic Initiation
Lucis Trust
Magic Words (Mantra)
Magic Circle
Magick
Man has Shadow
Man is a god
Mandela
Masons
Material Plane

Meditation
Merlin
Metaphysical
Metaphysics
Mind Control
Montessori Method
Moonies
Mother Kali
Muses
Music for Healing
Mystery Babylon
Mystical Christianity
Naturopathy
Nazism
Necromancy
Networking/Synergy
New Age Music
New Thinking/New Thought
Ninja
Oaths
Occult Toys and Games
Occult
Occult Numerology
Old Religion
Om
One is All
Oneness
Ongoing Incarnation
Orgone
Original Blessing
Ouija Boards
Paganism
Palmistry
Pantheism
Parapsychology
Past Life Analysis
Pegasus
Perennial Philosophy, The
Plan, The
Planetary Ascension

Planetary Commission
Planned Parenthood
Polarity Therapy
Population Control
Positive Confession
Positive Affirmation
Positive/Possibility Thinking
Positive Christianity
Power Animals
Prana
Presence, The
Pre-Christian
Primal Scream Therapy
Psychedelic
Psychiatry
Psychic Healing
Psychic Energy
Psychics/ESP
Purification/Cleansing of Earth
Pyramid Power
Quiet, The
Ra
Rainbow Bridge
Ram
Ramtha
Real Self
Reality, The
Rebirthing
Reconstructionism
Recycling of Spirits
Reflexology
Regression Therapy
Reincarnation
Religious Science
Restoration Theology
Right Brain/Left Brain Thinking
Rolfing
Rosicrucianism
Rune Stones
Sabbats

Sacred Sex
Sacred Earth
Sacred Psychology
Sai Baha
Sanat Kumara
Satan Worship
Satanic Day Care
Satanic Triangle
Satanic Pentagram
Saturn
Science of Mind
Scientology
Seances/Mediums
Secret Doctrine, The
Secular Humanism
Self-Love
Self-Realization
Seth Writings
Setsun
Sex Magick
Shakti
Shamanism
Shambhala
Shiva
Silva Mind Control
Sink Into Oneself
Solar Logos
Sorcerers
Soul Attunement
Spells
Spirit Helper
Spiritism
Spiritist
Spiritual Plane
Spiritualism
Stonehenge
Sufi Moslem
Sufism
Swastica
Sweat Lodges

Syncretism
Taliesin
Tantra
Tao
Taoism
Tapping In
Tarot Cards
Taste for Mystery
Tattoos
Thanatology
Theosophy
Third Eye
Thought-Forms
Trance State
Trancelike State
Transcendental Mediation (TM)
Transformation
Triangle within a Circle
Trilateral Commission
UFO's and Aliens
Ultimate Reality
Unicorn
Unitarianism
Unity Church
Universal Mind
Universal Consciousness
Universalism
Urantia Book, The
Values Clarification
Vedas
Vedic Scriptures
Vegetarianism
Vehicle (Spirit)
Vibrations/"Vibes"
Violet Flame, The
Virgo
Visualization
Visualize World Peace
Voodoo

Waldorf Schools
"What goes around comes
    around"
White Noise
White Brotherhood, The
White Magic
Whole Brain Learning
Witchcraft/Wicca
Witchdoctors
Wizards
Yin-Yang
Yoga
Zen

FOOTNOTES

PART I   THE LATE, GREAT CHRISTIAN FAMILY

1. Vera Stanley Alder, *When Humanity Comes of Age* (New York: Samuel Weiser, Inc., 1974), p. 190.
2. *Ibid.*, p. 62.
3. *Ibid.*, pp. 61-67.
4. *Ibid.*
5. *Ibid.*, p. 49.
6. *Ibid.*
7. *Ibid.*
8. Alice Bailey, *Education in the New Age* (New York: Lucis Trust Publishing, 1954), p. 80.
9. *Ibid.*, p. 70.
10. Vera Stanley Alder, *When Humanity Comes of Age*, p. 69.
11. Texe Marrs., *Dark Secrets of the New Age* (Westchester, IL: Crossway Books, 1987), pp. 177-188.
12. Benjamin Creme, *The Reappearance of the Christ and the Masters of Wisdom* (London: Tara Press, 1980), p. 89.
13. Foster Bailey, *Things to Come* (London: Lucis Trust Publishing, 1974), p. 38.
14. *Ibid.*, p. 34.
15. *Ibid.*
16. *Ibid.*
17. Quoted by Marilyn Ferguson in her book, *The Aquarian Conspiracy* (Los Angeles: J. P. Tarcher, Inc., 1980).
18. Martin Gross, *The Psychological Society* (New York: Simon & Schuster), p. 271.
19. *World's Most Precious Resource: It's Children* (Monograph, New York: World Goodwill), p. 31.
20. See *The Omega-Letter*, Toronto, Canada, April 11, 1988.
21. Barry McWaters, *Conscious Evolution* (San Francisco: Evolutionary Press, 1982), p. 113.
22. M. Scott Peck, *A Different Drum: Community Making and Peace* (New York: Simon & Schuster, 1987), p. 17.
23. *Ibid.*, p. 19.
24. *Ibid.*, p. 272.
25. *Ibid.*, p. 206.
26. *Ibid.*, p. 272.
27. *Ibid.*, p. 249.
28. *Ibid.*, p. 259.
29. Paul Vitz, *Psychology as Religion*, p. 61.
30. *Amerika* (TV series with actor Kris Kristofferson).
31. David Spangler, *Emergence: The Rebirth of the Sacred* (New York: Dell, 1984), p. 127.
32. Joshua Halpern, *Children of the Dawn* (Bodega, CA: Only with Love Publications, 1986), p. 3.

33. See *The Omega Letter*, May 1988, and *Gannet Westchester* newspaper, Jan. 23, 1988.
34. *Ibid.*
35. *For the Love of Children*, resource packet by the National Committee for the Prevention of Child Abuse, p. 16.
36. *Ibid.*, p. 17.
37. *Ibid.*, pp. 17-18.

PART II   THE BOLD NEW AGE CLAIM: CHRISTIAN PARENTS ARE IGNORANT, INSANE, UNSTABLE, UNFIT
1. *World's Most Precious Resource: It's Children* (New York: World Goodwill).
2. *Ibid.*
3. *Ibid.*
4. *Ibid.*, p. 8.
5. Bhagwan Rajneesh, quoted in *Mystery Mark of the New Age*, by Texe Marrs (Westchester, IL: Crossway Books, 1988), pp. 194-195.
6. Robert Anton Wilson, "The New Inquisition," *Meditation*, Winter 87-88, pp. 27-29.
7. Ruth Montgomery, *Ruth Montgomery: Herald of the New Age* (Golden City, NJ: Doubleday, 1986), p. 264; and see Montgomery's book, *Threshold to Tomorrow*.
8. *World's Most Precious Resource: It's Children*, p. 14.
9. *Ibid.*, p. 16.
10. *Ibid.*, p. 24.
11. *Ibid.*, pp. 16, 30.
12. *Ibid.*, p. 1.
13. Swami Muktananda, *Satsang With Baba* (India: Shree Gurudev Ashrang, 1978).
14. Robert Muller, *New Genesis* (Garden City, NY: Doubleday, 1984), p. 89.
15. *Ibid.*, p. 9.
16. *Ibid.*, pp. 127-128, 131-136.
17. *Ibid.*, pp. 127, 145.
18. *Ibid.*, p. 183.
19. Virginia Essene, *New Teachings for an Awakened Humanity* (Santa Clara, CA: Spiritual Education Company, 1986).
20. *Ibid.*, p. 165.
21. *Ibid.*, p. 170.
22. *Ibid.*, pp. 122-123.

PART III   THEY WANT OUR CHILDREN
1. David Spangler, *The New Age* (Issaquah, WA: Morningtown Press, 1988), pp. 36-37.
2. *Ibid.*, p. 38.
3. Elizabeth Clare Prophet, *Lord of the Seven Rays* (Livingston, MT: Summit University Press. 1986). p. 103.
4. *Ibid.*, p. 216.
5. *Ibid.*
6. *Ibid.*, p. 230.
7. *Ibid.*

8. *Ibid.*, p. 233.
9. *Ibid.*, p. 232.
10. Elizabeth Clare Prophet, *My Soul Doth Magnify the Lord* (Livingston, MT: Summit University Press, 1986), p. ix.
11. *Ibid.*
12. *Ibid.*, p. iv.
13. *Ibid.*, p. vi.
14. *Ibid.*, p. x.
15. *Ibid.*, p. xv.
16. *Ibid.*, p. xvii.
17. *Ibid.*, p. 240.
18. *Ibid.*, p. 232.
19. *Ibid.*, p. 233.
20. Alice Bailey, *The Reappearance of the Christ* (New York: Lucis Trust Publishing , 1948; renewed 1976; tenth printing, 1984).
21. *Ibid.*
22. Benjamin Creme, *Messages From Maitreya the Christ* (Los Angeles: Tara Center, 1980).
23. *Ibid.*
24. Vera Alder, *The Fifth Dimension* (New York: Samuel Weiser, Inc.), p. 131.
25. *Ibid.*, pp. 128-129.
26. *Ibid.*, pp. 146-147.
27. *Ibid.*, p. 147.
28. *Ibid.*, pp. 152-153.
29. *Ibid.*, p. 154.
30. *Ibid.*, p. 122.
31. *Ibid.*
32. Virginia Essene, *New Teachings for an Awakening Humanity.*
33. *Ibid.*, p. 158.
34. *Ibid.*, p. 165.
35. *Ibid.*, p. 158.
36. *Ibid.*, p. 157.
37. *Ibid.*
38. Herbert Puryear, Ph.D., *Sex and the Spiritual Path* (New York: Bantam Books, 1986), p. 114.
39. *Ibid.*, pp. 114-115.
40. *Ibid.*
41. Foster Bailey, *Running God's Plan* (New York: Lucis Trust Publishing), p. 65.
42. *Ibid.*, p. 69.
43. Paula Tyler, *New Age Metaphysics: An Introduction for Young Adults* (Eureka Springs, AR: Metaphysical Enterprises, 1987), pp. 10-11.
44. Omraam Aivankov, *Aquarius: Herald of the New Age*, Vol. 25.
45. *Ibid.*
46. *Ibid.*
47. *Ibid.*

About the Author

Texe Marrs is author of over 25 books, including books on high tech and other subjects for such major publishers as Simon & Schuster, Dow Jones-Irwin, John Wiley, and Prentice Hall. Three of his Christian books have been #1 (non-fiction) on the national bestseller's list. A career U.S. Air Force officer (retired), he taught American defense policy at the University of Texas at Austin for five years, and has taught international affairs and political science for two other universities.

Texe Marrs' newsletter, *Flashpoint*, is distributed throughout the U.S.A. and Canada and in over 40 foreign countries around the world.

For Our Free Newsletter

Texe Marrs publishes a highly acclaimed newsletter about Bible prophecy, the New Age Movement, cults, the occult challenge to Christianity, and other important topics.

If you would like to receive, *absolutely free,* a subscription to this fascinating newsletter, please write to:

Living Truth Ministries
8103-A Shiloh Court
Austin, Texas 78745